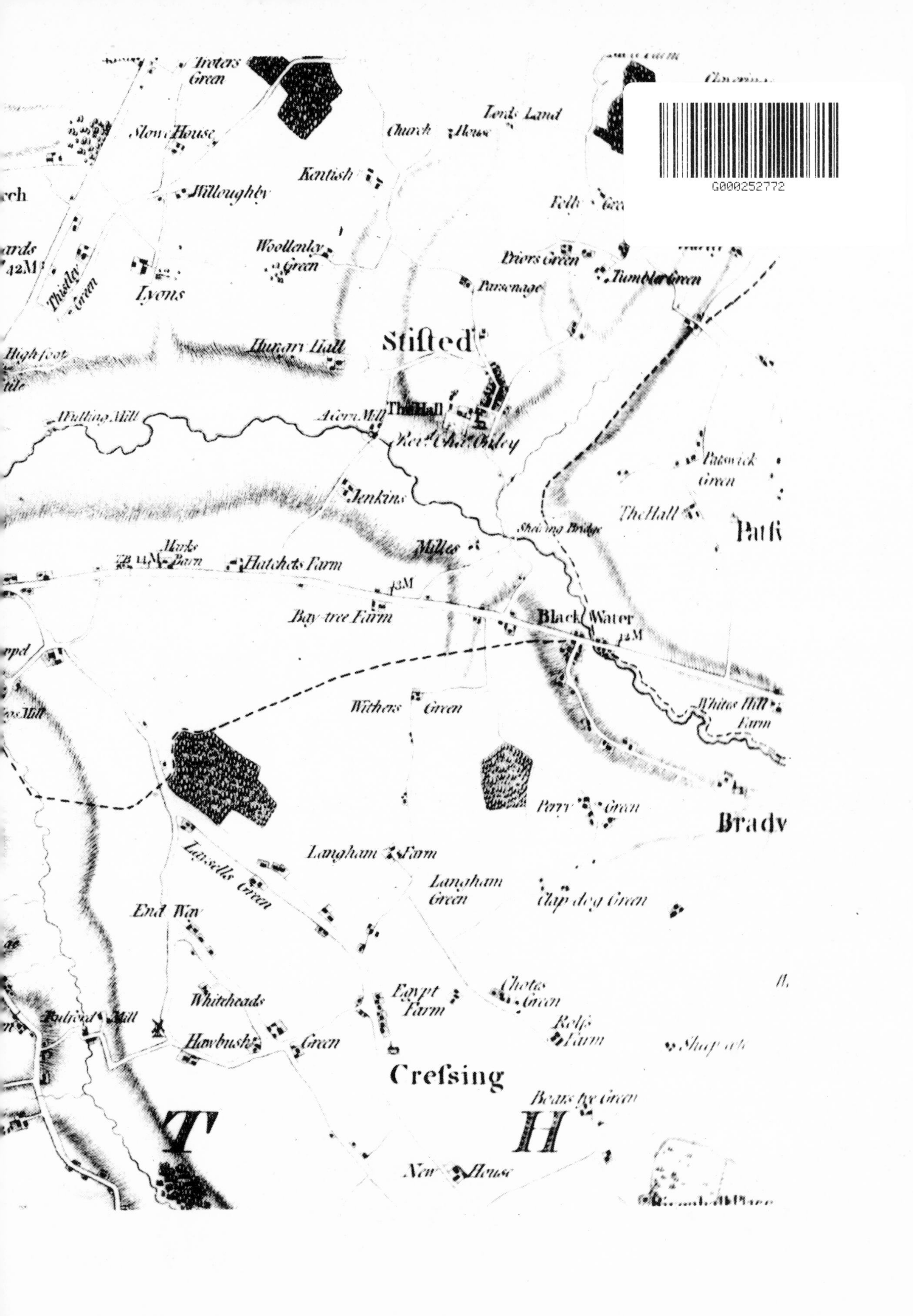

Treters Green
Slow House
Church House
Lords Land
Kentish
Willoughby
Woollenly Green
Priors Green
Tumbler Green
Parsonage
Thistley Green
Lyons
42M
Stifted
High foot
A Fulling Mill
A Corn Mill
The Hall
Revd Chas Onley
Jenkins
Patswick Green
The Hall
Milles
Marks Barn
Hatchets Farm
13M
Bay tree Farm
Black Water
Withers Green
Whites Hill Farm
Perry Green
Langham Farm
Langham Green
Lassells Green
Clap dog Green
End Way
Whiteheads
Egypt Farm
Chotes Green
Rolfs Farm
Hawbush Green
Crefsing
Bears tye Green
T
H
New House

The Book of Braintree and Bocking 1981
has been published as a Limited
Edition of which this is

Number 401

A complete list of the
original subscribers is
printed at the back of the book

THE BOOK OF BRAINTREE AND BOCKING

COVER: ABOVE—Braintree and Bocking Chamber of Trade, 1979, by Albany Wiseman. (VL) BELOW—Braintree Market, 1826. Commissioned by Thomas Nottidge, descendant of a family of baymakers, from Robert Crane. (VL)

ABOVE: St Michael's, engraved in 1818, (ERO/JA) and BELOW: St Mary's Bocking, engraved in 1816. (ERO/JA)

THE BOOK OF BRAINTREE & BOCKING

BY

MICHAEL BAKER BA

BARRACUDA BOOKS LIMITED
BUCKINGHAM, ENGLAND
MCMLXXXI

PUBLISHED BY BARRACUDA BOOKS LIMITED
BUCKINGHAM, ENGLAND
AND PRINTED BY
HOLYWELL PRESS LIMITED
OXFORD, ENGLAND

BOUND BY
WEATHERBY WOOLNOUGH
WELLINGBOROUGH, ENGLAND

JACKET PRINTED BY
CHENEY & SONS LIMITED
BANBURY, OXON

LITHOGRAPHY BY
OXFORD LITHO PLATES LIMITED
OXFORD, ENGLAND

DISPLAY SET IN BASKERVILLE
AND TEXT SET IN 12/14 pt BASKERVILLE
BY BRIAN ROBINSON
NORTH MARSTON, ENGLAND

ISBN 0 86023 134 8

Contents

Acknowledgements

This book could not have appeared without help from a great many people. I owe my interest in the subject to my father's own work in local history studies and to 21 years spent in the town. It has been sharpened by the work of Braintree's earlier historians, notably John Cunnington and Alfred Hills.

I owe a great debt to the many people who have unfolded their memories to me. Also to the staff at the Essex Record Office who have been generous with their time in making both written and pictorial archives available. I am grateful, too, to the County Archivist, Mr Gray, for his permission to reproduce many of the illustrations.

John Armistead and his camera came to my help at the eleventh hour and I am grateful to him for his speed and for the quality of the photographs. For further illustrations I am indebted to Nicki Gowers of the *Braintree and Witham Times,* to Hester Bury of the Warner Archive, and to everyone else who gave or loaned items.

Vic Lewis and the Chamber of Trade kindly allowed me to reproduce the 'modern' version of the Market Print—a few of which are, I am told, still available. My thanks also to Mr Makin and Mr Peacock and to Chrissy Robathan who drew the maps and sketches.

My relatives in Braintree have kindly endured my many visits. Braintree library, Mr Joscelyne, and the Braintree and Bocking Heritage Trust provided the subscription facilities.

Finally, it remains only to thank the publisher and the subscribers for their faith, and to admit sole responsibility for any errors.

Dedication

For my parents and Chrissy for their encouragement.

Foreword

by Malcolm Bryan, Braintree District Councillor
and Chairman of the Braintree and Bocking Heritage Trust

It gives me great pleasure to write this foreword to Michael Baker's *Book of Braintree and Bocking.* This book will be warmly welcomed by all who love the town and who are interested in its historical development.

Few English rural towns can have witnessed such a long and varied procession of peoples and events. These have included: Bronze Age settlements; Roman military might; Aetheric, the Saxon chieftain who divided the land which became Braintree and Bocking; the granting of the market charter by King John; a unique system of local government; the hostelries and revelry of the pilgrim travellers in the middle ages; the development of a renowned woollen industry; rich clothiers and colourful fairs; the birthplace of internationally famous firms such as Courtaulds and Crittalls; down to the people and events of our present times.

In the past little of this rich story has been publicly displayed or set down in written and illustrated form. Thankfully this situation is now changing and Michael Baker's thorough research and love of his subject have produced a book full of interest written in a style which absorbs the attention of the reader.

Through this book many people will become more actively involved in the history of the town and come to value and cherish its unique past.

Malcolm Bryan

Preface

by J. Corley, Chairman of the Braintree and Bocking Local History Society

For long regarded as a small unimportant place buried in rural Essex, Braintree has been rather neglected by the historian while incorrect statements, often repeated by successive authors, have sometimes fostered inaccurate ideas about the town.

Now in this *Book of Braintree* we are fortunate to have a serious study of the town by a scholar who has made excellent use of the many documents and papers available, especially in the Essex Record Office, to produce a detailed history of Braintree and Bocking.

So we can now enjoy this study of the town from the days of the earliest pre-historic settlement, through the Roman period, then into Saxon and manorial times when its population was concentrated in the area about Chapel Hill. For centuries after those days both Braintree and Bocking were famed for their woollen cloth, a manufacture replaced in the 19th century by an equally famous silk industry while the end of the same century saw the rise of noted engineers whose products have spread the name Braintree throughout the world.

Recent years have seen the rise of industrial estates with their highly specialised trades, yet Braintree still maintains its name as one of the most attractive market centres in Essex and for which it has been famous since the 12th century.

This volume will be much appreciated by the residents of the town and district and by all those interested in the ever more popular study of local history.

J. Corley

A Friendly caution to all **Malsters, Millers, & other dealers in Corn**.

Observe my woful case, & view it well
And learn from me to Buy, as well as Sell
W–NG'd with too eager haste at getting gain,
T-ff-n I cheated, & ill treated P-yne,
L-ns-ll, & L-ke, & half a hundred more,
They all condemn me on the Roguish score
The parent Widow & her Offspring call
Aloud for vengeance on my head to fall,
The pig I forced to Market with my own
Scream'd out you Rascal all the way to Town
My odious Name has been so bad accounted
I'm thus degraded, & as ill am mounted.
My Foes I find they would not grudge the cost
To see me drench'd, or in a Blanket tost
But see above my Just deserts appear
The pill'ry & the Gallows both are near
Yet am I hardned & will onward go
Tho' ev'ry honest Man become my Foe
And Roguery & Rags compleat my Overthrow

A libel pinned to the Pump in the Market Place, c1770. This led to legal action by Mr Wing against Mr Tiffin. (ERO/CR)

ABOVE: Roman soldiers: Town Hall mural by Grieffenhagen. (ERO/JA).
BELOW: The site of 'Braintree X-Roads' early this century. (ERO/JA)

Braintree X-Roads

Travellers on the road from Chelmsford to Braintree may be puzzled by the road sign marked 'Braintree X-Roads'. For this junction has been rather obscured in recent years, not least by the town's one-way system. Yet the crossroads is probably the most important landmark in the long history of Braintree. Almost 2,000 years ago, Stane Street—which joined the two major Roman towns of Colchester and St Albans—was crossed by a military way from Chelmsford to Gosfield.

The new road was probably a response to the need to move soldiers swiftly into East Anglia following Boadicea's revolt and attack on Colchester. An important crossroads would almost certainly have had a fort to protect it, although no archaeological evidence has been found to reveal its location. It would have been a busy spot. Soldiers marching from London crossed the path of carts, heavily laden with grain, bumping their way along Stane Street. As people began to make their homes here, a small Romano-British town grew up to the south-west of the road junction.

The buildings were mostly wooden, although a few had the luxury of window glass. The recent discovery of several objects—a manicure set, a palette of Purbeck marble, and some fine pottery and ornaments—suggests that some of the inhabitants lived gracefully. The Romans introduced enormous changes to the rural settlements of East Anglia and, when their occupation of Britain ended, c430 AD, their ways had been widely accepted by the native population.

There had been people living in the Braintree area long before the Romans arrived. A considerable amount of Bronze Age material has been found locally, and it seems probable that the Chapel Hill-Skitts Hill part of the present town has been inhabited since at least the fifth century BC. The people of the Bronze and, later, Iron Ages built their homes on the lower ground of the river vallies, in this case the Brain Valley.

In the pre-Roman period, these 'people of the river' were able to work iron and to fashion it into rough tools. The Trinovantes, as they are known, were peaceful farmers, living in scattered huts, who tilled the light sandy soils and hunted wild animals in the surrounding forests.

It was the arrival of the Romans which changed this pattern of living. The Romano-British town was built on a sandy ridge close to the chief roads. The lack of natural protection was not serious while Roman soldiers were present, but after they had gone the town was vulnerable to new invaders. These were Germanic tribes who swooped in small bands, following the rivers inland. One of these tribes—the East Saxons—settled in the area to which they have given the name 'Essex'. They ruled here for nearly three centuries, during which time the town at the crossroads was almost forgotten. For the Saxons, fearing attack, built their homes away from the main Roman roads. Turning

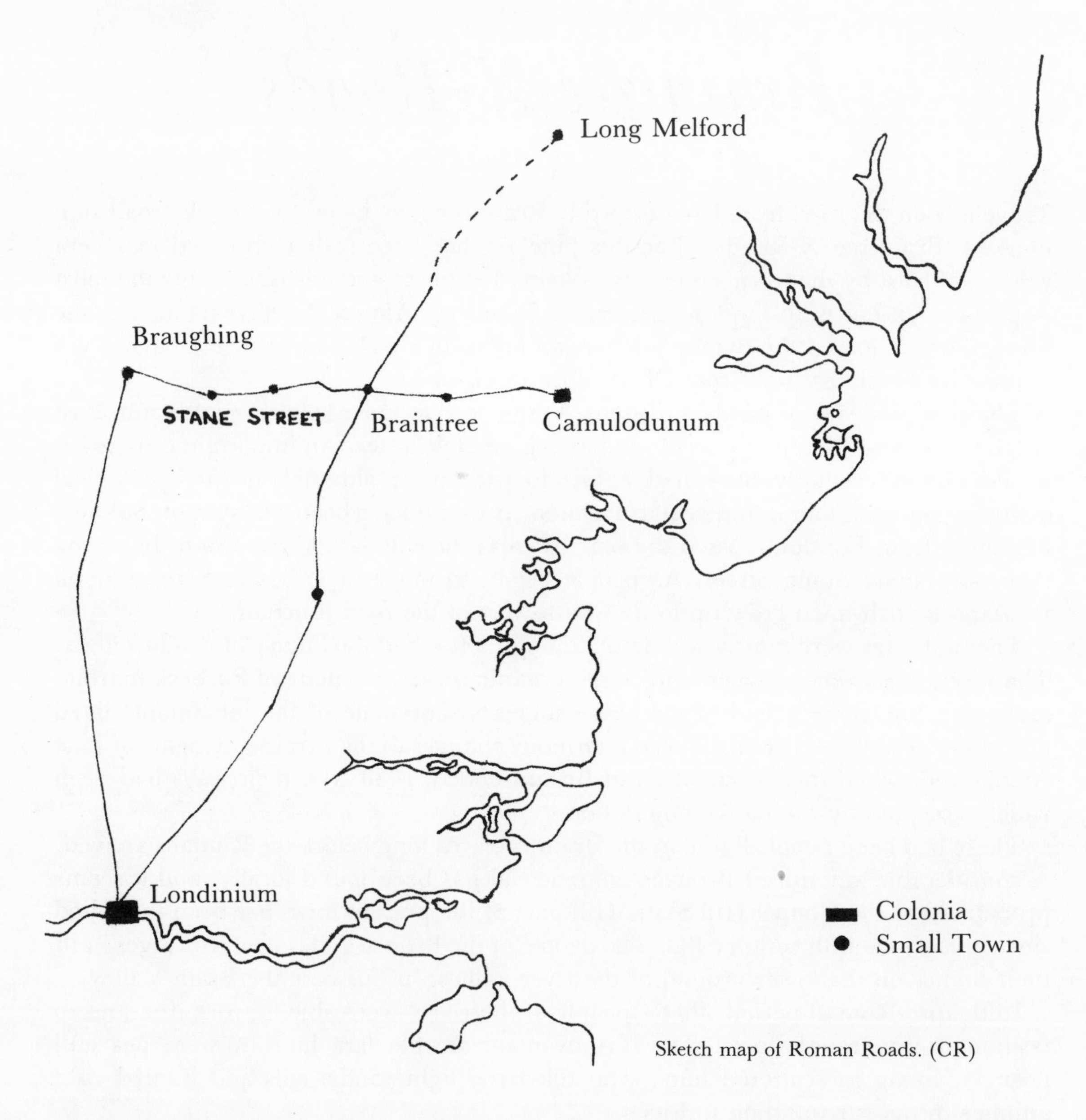

Sketch map of Roman Roads. (CR)

their backs upon the Romano-British town, they created a settlement around a water-mill and a chapel to the east of the crossroads, in the area now known as Chapel Hill.

The final years of Saxon rule were characterised by constant battles with the invading Danes and Vikings. One of the most celebrated was fought just a few miles

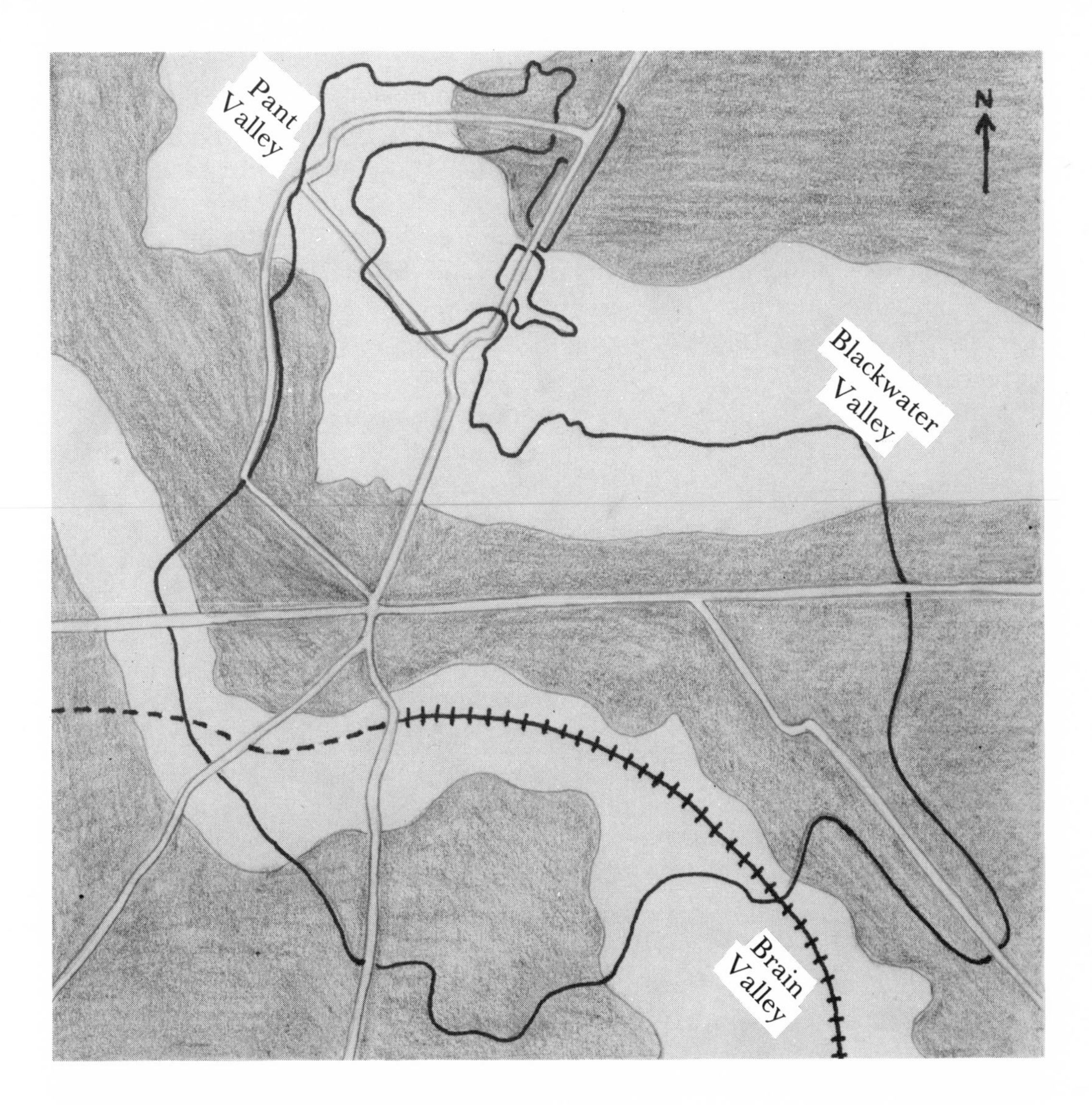

Sketch map of Braintree's topography. (CR)

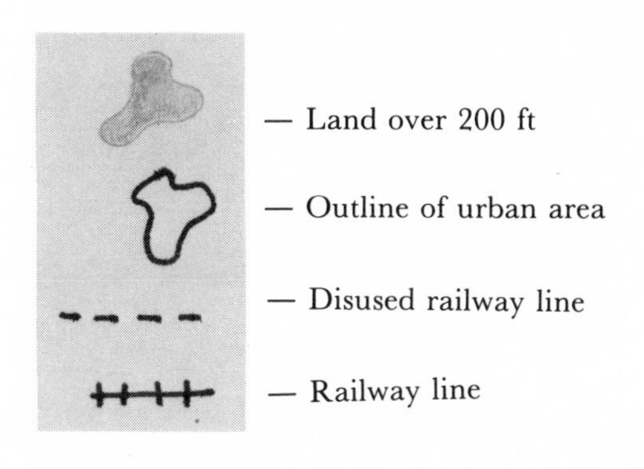

— Land over 200 ft

— Outline of urban area

— Disused railway line

— Railway line

from Braintree, at Maldon, in 991. The old English poem, *The Battle of Maldon*, relates how a Saxon nobleman named Aetheric fought with particular ferocity. Aetheric owned most of the land in the present parishes of Braintree and Bocking, and it seems likely that it was he who marched with a band of men from the Braintree settlement to turn back the Scandinavian invaders. But the battle was lost, and Aetheric died from the wounds he received. In his will he left his Braintree lands to the Bishop of London, who became the lord of the manor. At the same time, his Bocking lands went to the Prior and monks of Canterbury. It is perhaps worth mentioning here, that the right to nominate the Dean of St Mary's Church, Bocking, remains with the Archbishop of Canterbury to this day.

By the mid-11th century, there was a community of considerable size on the Bishop of London's estate at Chapel Hill. This estate would almost certainly have had a church at a fairly early date, and there is evidence of a chapel in this area whose ruins survived into the 19th century. A painting of these ruins in 1849 pictured 'a view of the part of the chapel then standing, showing the west end with a triplet of three equal lancet lights surmounted by a triangle all moulded with stone, the body of the wall of flint rubble—a high pitched gable and angle buttresses'.

At the time of the Domesday Survey, completed in 1086, the community at Chapel Hill was far more important than the settlement close to the crossroads. The name of this larger community appears to have been 'Raines', which, it has been suggested, derived from the Celtic name for the river Brain, or possibly from two Saxon words meaning 'near the river'. The Domesday entry says Raines was held by Bishop William and, at the time of Edward the Confessor's reign in 1066, covered 'four hides and 30 acres' (a 'hide' was about 60 to 120 acres). There was a water-mill, and two ploughs belonged to the lord of the manor and five to the men. The manor included woodland for 200 swine and 16 acres of meadow, and 16 'villeins' and four 'serfs' worked the lord of the manor's lands.

The name Braintree first appears in the Domesday Book as 'Branchetreu', but this refers only to the area roughly to the west and south-west of the crossroads, the general location of the previous Romano-British town. Here, three 'free men' held some 30 acres. Branchetreu, which passed through several different spellings before it became Braintree, is thought to derive from 'treo(w)', an Old English word for tree, and 'Branoc', a personal name.

From the Town Hall Murals: ABOVE: Battle of Maldon, 991. Danes attacking the Saxons. (ERO/JA) BELOW: Ploughing, sowing and harrowing c1060. (ERO/JA)

ABOVE: King John presents the market charter to the Bishop of London, c1199. From Town Hall Murals. (ERO/JA) BELOW: St Michael's seen from Notley Road, 1832. (JA)

Mediaeval Town

For more than 100 years after the Domesday Survey, Raines continued to hold its position as the more important of the two communities, but, at the end of the 12th century, an important decision was taken which was to reverse these roles. The lord of the manor of Raines, William de St Maria, the Bishop of London, had applied to King John for permission to hold a market. The market charter was granted c1199, and with it, provision was made for an annual cattle and horse fair on 2 October.

The best site for a market, though, was not on Chapel Hill, but at the crossroads nearer the traffic. The first Market Place was created to the east of the crossroads, on the site now known as Little Square, bounded on the north by Swan Side and on the east by Drury Lane. The layout of the stalls has probably survived in the existing rows of buildings, now separated by the Drury Lane 'gants' or alleys. So, a 'new town' was born, a town whose centre-piece was the market square and whose prosperity depended on shopkeepers and stall-holders rather than on tilling the soil.

As the new emerged, so the old went into decline. The Chapel Hill community lost ground steadily as the market grew. An anonymous 19th century poet described this dramatic change of fortunes in rhyming couplets:

'About the time the Norman came
Old Branchetreu claimed a sep'rate name;
For then it was that Raines declined,
And to the branching town resigned
All hope of ever being great.
So, from that time full slow but sure
One town in size grew more and more;
The other, effortless, decayed,
Nor could fatality evade.
And while old Raines fell thus away,
So fell her church in like decay:
Its age-riven walls of flint and stone
Crumbled, to fall uncared, unknown.'

The fate of the chapel on Chapel Hill, once perhaps the parish church, mirrors the demise of Raines. Soon after 1199, the new parish church of St Michael's was founded and the chapel became subservient to it. Although the chapel remained in use for many years, it was in ruins by the 19th century and now no trace survives. A similar fate befell the Bishop's palace, the manor house, and the parsonage which all stood nearby. The last bishop to live here was Nicholas Ridley who was Bishop of London in 1550 when the manor passed out of ecclesiastical hands. By the 18th century, though, it appears to have gone. Newcourt, an ecclesiastical historian, writing in 1710 reports: '...and of all that was upon this manor, there now remains only the Mill, at present called "Bacon's Mill", which stands upon a little stream at the foot of that hill, which was formerly crowned with the Bishop's Palace'.

The new church met not only the demands of the growing local population, but also served the stream of pilgrims who passed through the town on their way to shrines in Suffolk and Norfolk. As the market grew in importance and the town became known as a stopping-place for those on pilgrimages, prosperity arrived. The demand for services ranging from inns and stabling to saddlers and brewers turned Braintree into a busy, noisy and somewhat disordered place. By 1364, a visitor noted that Braintree was 'a great populous towne, and a Market-towne, having in it to the number of 480 houseling people and more'. A few years earlier, in 1346, Braintree had been considered sufficiently prosperous to supply four armed foot-soldiers for Edward III's army at Crecy. This gives some indication of the town's importance compared to the other larger towns in Essex, such as Chelmsford which also sent four, Colchester (20), and Saffron Waldon (6).

The town grew outwards from the Market Place—which remained in Drury Lane until the early 1600s—and the frontage of Bank Street was filled during the late 14th and early 15th centuries. Many buildings from this period survived into the present century, only to be obliterated by shop-front development. The area of the present High Street witnessed the next stage of building, the first houses being built before the end of the 15th century, on what may have been part of the former burial ground of St Michael's Church.

The town's growth was not continuous. Like everywhere else, the population was prey to the intermittent ravages of the plague, in particular the Black Death, which wiped out one third of the population of England. Also, the market alone would not have been enough to sustain growth. But a new industry had taken root in Braintree some time in the early 14th century. This was the cloth trade, which, during the following years, brought great wealth to several local families, established a manufacturing tradition in the town, and helped bring the twin-townships of Braintree and Bocking closer together. In particular it created the wealth for the enlargement of the church and for the building of the fine clothiers' homes which line Bradford Street.

The cloth trade raised both Braintree and Bocking to a position of importance in the county. In 1594, Norden the Essex historian wrote: 'There are within this shire these especiall clothing towns—Colchester, Coggeshall, Braintree, Bocking, and Dedham'. It also created a class of wealthy clothiers who joined the ranks of successful tradesmen from which the town's governing group was almost exclusively drawn. Surviving wills show that some of the town's tradesmen became very wealthy. When Nicholas

Wilbore, a Braintree draper, died in 1582 he left his family a shop and a stall in the Market Place, a house called the 'Chequer', a house in the 'Gant' called 'Halls Grove', a meadow at Skitts Hill, a field at Bocking End, and other lands in Bocking and Stisted. Other wills reveal some of the occupations of Braintree's middling-classes: a butcher, a tanner, and the landlord of the George Inn which stood in Bank Street.

The emergence of a 'respectable' group of townsmen, who had an interest in maintaining the social order, came at a time when the growing community was often rough and disorderly. Throughout the early 1600s the disorders of the market and the annual fair were symptomatic of the unruliness of the town's inhabitants and visitors. In 1620, when the fair threatened to get out of hand, the Vicar of St Michael's, Samuel Collins, was forced to ask the then lord of the manor, the Earl of Warwick, 'to reform the disorders of the fair'. The fair-time high spirits, no doubt reinforced by large doses of Braintree beer, had overflowed the three days allowed by the charter. 'Bear-baiting, fencing, and the like' were still being merrily enjoyed in the streets and were causing 'great hindrance' to the more sober tradesmen of the town.

The Braintree Fair must have produced a colourful scene for in 1626 the constables gathered £3 12s 6d for offences of swearing and drunkenness. The following year they collected £3 2s 5d for the same offences, which perhaps indicates a slight improvement in the morals of the townspeople. To add to the noise made by the locals, there were the itinerant ballad-singers. So popular were these strolling entertainers that 'Out-Roaring Dick' and 'Wit Wimbas' could make, so it was said, as much as 20 shillings a day.

With all this revelling, Braintree might have fallen into a drunken demise if there had not been someone to take control of the town's affairs. Samuel Collins, the clergyman who solicited the aid of the Earl of Warwick, was such a man. He became vicar of St Michael's in 1610, where he stayed until 1658. From the start he took a firm grasp of the church and parish. He began by reforming the Select Vestry, the body made up of the vicar, churchwardens and prominent citizens which provided Braintree's first local government. There had been a Select Vestry at Braintree for a long time. The Essex historian, Muilman, writing in 1772, noted 'in the parish there has been since time immemorial, a select vestry for the business of the parish, consisting of 24 in number'.

From their constant membership of 24, the select vestry took the name of the 'Company of Four and Twenty'. The social historians, Beatrice and Sidney Webb, in their major study *English Local Government*, cited the '4 & 20' as a classic example of early select vestry government, describing them as 'a curious body half-way between guild and municipal court of Aldermen'. The exact date of the first meeting of the '4 & 20' is not known. However, they were certainly governing the town from at least 1565, when William Skinner, one of the Company, was buried. In these early years the Company was known variously as the 'Headboroughs', the 'Governors of the Town', and the 'Town Magistrates'.

In 1611, the Company appealed to the Bishop of London for his help in keeping troublesome intruders out of the town. The following year, the Bishop responded by granting the '4 & 20' his official warrant to run the town and to elect new members themselves. Samuel Collins put the Company on an efficient footing by drawing up a new set of rules, 27 of them in all. The first required the members to meet 'in an orderly manner in cloaks and gowns on the first Monday in each month, at 10 o'clock, notice being given by the Sexton tolling the great bell ten strokes'. Other rules provided for voting by secret ballot and for a system of fines for failure to be silent, using 'scornful revilings', and failing to sign the minutes. The meetings began with prayers—the fine for latecomers being 6d—and ended with dinner at the house of each member in turn.

Although 'open' vestry meetings of ordinary parishioners were also held at about this time, they had little influence or power. Only very rarely did the open meeting pass a resolution, and then only on minor matters such as the scale of fees levied for burials. The Bishop of London did not approve of this sort of democracy. He referred to the Select Vestry as the 'better and ancienter sort of the parish' and referred to the intrusion of the ordinary people as 'an inconvenience'. There was no semblance of democracy or representation about the Select Vestry. It was a self-electing body, which when vacancies occurred—'as a result of decay, removal, death, or by scandalous living, drunkenness, whoredom, or other evil life'—chose in secret whom to invite into its ranks. They obviously took a great deal of pride in their public position and formed an exclusive social oligarchy. They even set aside a pew in church for themselves and their families.

Yet, under Collins' rigorous leadership, the '4 & 20' did much to make Braintree a better place to live, though often at the expense of the 'less respectable'. Under the Elizabethan Poor Laws every parish tried to keep its number of paupers to a minimum. Braintree took extreme steps in appointing a Beadle in 1623 'to keep strangers out and to gather up about supper time all that begg at men's doors'. The '4 & 20' walked the town in pairs, reporting on the unemployed, 'excluding undesirables', and drawing up a list of those 'journeymen who live in the town contrary to the law' and those who fail to attend church. They also kept an eye open for sexual wantonness, less out of a concern for public morality than a desire to save the parish the cost of any illegitimate children. Their snooping gave rise to occasional reports as: 'Notice is given of one Grace that is out of service that keeps at Little's of Bocking that was seen privately in a chamber locked up with Joseph Pullen'.

They were, in effect, benevolent despots, insisting on conformity, yet bearing a great weight of social work as constables, churchwardens, overseers, and surveyors. They repaired bridges, bought fire-engines, restricted ale-licences, stocked the town's arsenal, and ordered 'that the chief streets of this town be kept cleaner for all the countrie shall be shamed of it'. The Company also administered aid to the poor. They ran the 'hospital' or poorhouse which stood between New Street and the field which is now Market Square. Orphans, widows, the elderly and the sick were housed here and given tasks to earn their keep. Food, clothes, and firewood were also given to some of the poor in their own homes.

The '4 & 20' could not have had a more difficult time than during the unsettled 17th century. They had to supply horses and soldiers to Parliament during the Civil War, and the town itself was nearly caught in the middle of a battle. In 1648, Royalist troops marched on Braintree, where they arrived on the evening of 10 June. On their way they had taken Leighs Priory, the home of the Earl of Warwick, where they had captured '2 Grass Field-pieces, 2-300 muskets and the same number of pikes, and a quantity of match and ball, and some barrels of powder'. By the time they reached Braintree the army was four thousand strong, including six hundred cavalry.

Two Parliamentary armies were in hot pursuit. While the Royalists were at Braintree, these were at Coggeshall and Chelmsford respectively. Braintree was caught between the two, with the prey camped in the town. The local inhabitants had little sleep that night, wondering whether they would wake up in the middle of a battleground or a siege. The next day, the Royalists assembled for prayers and then made a break for Colchester. There the Parliamentary forces caught up with them and the long and famous Colchester siege ensued.

The return of peace brought little relief to the town. The final decades of the 17th century were hard years. In 1664, the Reverend Kidder of Rayne referred to the local people as 'factious to the greatest degree'. The misery was deepened by a devastating visitation of the plague. Six hundred and sixty five people died in Braintree—a third of the population—while only 22 were visited by the plague and survived. Trade fell off as nervous tradesmen, carriers, and merchants avoided the town. Grass began to sprout in the main streets.

With decline came revolt. In 1682, four Constables appointed by the Court Leet—a court held by the lord of the manor—refused to render their accounts to the '4 & 20'. The Company responded by taking their case to the Quarter Sessions. The verdict went against them, and the Justices ordered that other people were entitled to be present at the annual rendering of the accounts. This was a major blow to the exclusivity and pride of the Company. In 1711 matters came to a head once again. This time no compromise could be reached. Within two years, by order of the Quarter Sessions, the 'closed' vestry came to an end with the replacement of co-option by open elections. This was the end of the '4 & 20'; meetings became irregular and were poorly attended,after 1716 no further record of the 'Company of Four and Twenty'exists.

They had served the town well; most select vestries were corrupt by the 18th century, yet, according to Braintree's 19th century historian, Cunnington, 'there was no sign of corruption, partiality, or jobbery at Braintree'. These sentiments were echoed by the Webbs whose study of the Company ended with these words: 'From first to last we see no trace of corruption...The members even paid out of their own pockets for their monthly dinner and were evidently always subscribing money for charitable objects. At no little expense of time and money to themselves, this little company of "ancients" fulfilled what they doubtless felt as their obligation to give both deliberative and executive service in the administration of their community'.

The 'gant' leading to LEFT: St Michael's; (ERO/JA) ABOVE: George Yard, and BELOW: leading from George Yard.

LEFT: Little Square, c1900. (ERO/JA) RIGHT; The Six Bells and central figure of 'Old Harkilees'.

Six Bells Corner, Bocking, c1900. A hostel for pilgrims is believed to have stood nearby. (ERO/JA)

ABOVE: Bradford Street towards Bocking Mill. (ERO/JA) BELOW: Bank Street looking north. c1900. (ERO/JA)

ABOVE: High Street looking towards Fuller's, the bootmakers. (NG)
BELOW: Bocking Mill, c1900. (NG)

A fulling mill, from Chapman & André's Map of Essex, 1777. (ERO/JA)
INSET: Robert, Earl of Warwick. (ERO/JA)

Bays and Says

Few towns can match Braintree's lengthy tradition of manufacturing. Looking back, there is a long line of continuity from the metal-working industries of this century, through the manufacture of silk in the 19th century, and on to the craft workshops of a busy 18th century market-town. But the foundations of manufacturing industry in the town were laid around the 14th century with the woollen cloth trade.

By the late 1300s, English clothiers were beginning to rival their counterparts in the Netherlands in the making of fine cloth, as shown by Chaucer's 'Wife of Bath':

> 'Of clooth-making she hadde swiche an haunt
> She passed hem of Ypres and of Gaunt...'.

Certainly by 1452 the Braintree Bailiffs 'certified that the art or mystery of weaving woollen cloth was exercised there and more so than any other arts or mysteries and had been from time beyond memory'.

An art—in the original sense of the word—it most certainly was, for the process was made up of a complex set of skills. The work was not carried out in one place, nor were the employees working on the clothiers' premises. Instead the clothier was a middleman who bought the raw wool, then delivered it to a succession of skilled workers, who worked in their own homes. These included, in turn, woolbeaters, woolcombers, spinners, and weavers. Each stage of activity was carried out in a different location, often out of town. The spinners lived mostly in surrounding villages such as Stisted or Cressing, whereas the weavers almost all lived in either Braintree or Bocking.

The clothier would put out his work and set a date by which it was to be ready for collection. Once the cloth was woven, the clothier took it to be fulled at the water-mills on the river Brain at Chapel Hill, and on the river Pant-Blackwater at Bradford Street and Church Street, Bocking. Then it was stretched on tenterhooks (hence the expression 'to be on tenterhooks'), roughened with teazles, and the surface cut smooth by shearmen. Finally the finished cloth was stored at the clothier's barn before being sent to London either by wagon or by sea from Maldon.

About the time of the Reformation, in the early 16th century, the Braintree and Bocking clothiers began to specialise in the manufacture of a finer type of cloth brought over by Flemish weavers who settled in this part of Essex. These were the 'new draperies', known as bays and says, referred to in the old saying:

'Hops, reformation, bays, and beer,
Came into England all in a year'.

These bays had a worsted warp and woollen weft, and says were similar except that they had a twill-weave. The chief market for the bays and says from the Braintree area was abroad, particularly Spain and Portugal.

The fortunes of the cloth trade are reflected in the history of one street in particular. Bradford Street was on the route taken by the pilgrims following the old Roman road from London to Bury St Edmunds. It seems likely that there was a hostel where the pilgrims could stay overnight near where the Six Bells now stands. But it was when the clothiers moved into Bradford Street that the road became a centre of importance and activity.

There were a number of Wool Halls here, where weekly sales of yarn and cloth took place. Closeness to the fulling mills in Bocking and to the skilled workforce of both towns provided the street's main attraction in the clothiers' eyes. The fine houses which line both sides of the street are testimony to the fortunes amassed by them. They were usually family businesses, passed on from father to son, and they established the local fame of a number of surnames.

Several of these families became the rural gentry of the 18th century when, as the cloth trade collapsed, they switched their fortunes to farming. As Defoe observed, in the early 18th century 'many of the great families who now pass for gentry...have originally been raised from this noble manufacture'. The Ruggles of Bradford House moved from the cloth trade to agriculture when they bought a large country estate in Finchingfield. The Nottages, five generations of whom lived at Fulling Mill House (now the Convent), became landowners on a large scale and became partners in the 19th century Sparrow's Bank. Other families who moved from the cloth trade to the land-owning gentry were the Savills and Englishes, both of Bocking, and the Peers and Windles of Braintree.

By the early years of the 17th century, the cloth trade had helped to turn Braintree into a busy and thriving town. In 1620, more than 600 bays were being sent from the town each week. Alongside the manufacture of cloth, the market continued to grow and to provide jobs, saving the town from a dangerous overdependence on a single industry. This, though, had happened at Bocking where, by the end of the century, 148 out of 158 apprenticeships were in the cloth trade.

The cloth trade reached its peak in the middle of the 17th century. Yet it was not without its depressions. One of the worst came in the 1620s, when the export of cloth fell to two-thirds its normal level. The first Royal Commission ever set up to inquire into the causes of unemployment was created in 1622. By 1629 things had still not improved. In April of that year 200 Braintree and Bocking weavers marched to the court of the Quarter Sessions at Chelmsford to present a petition. They complained of 'extreme necessity and disability to maintain and relieve themselves and their families'.

When no action was taken, the desperate weavers appealed directly to the King. Their letter was dated 8 May, 1629:

> 'To the King's Most Excellent Majesty
> The humble petition of the Weavers of Bocking and Braintree in the County of Essex and the neighbouring towns thereabouts to the number of One Hundred Thousand with them which doe depend upon them.
>
> Humbly shewing that the trade hath been decaying for this seven years or thereabouts to their utter undoing, Now they have no work at all, by reason whereof they...their wives, and their children, are like to perish, for in this declining time they are not able to subsist any longer by reason of the abatement of their wages...these being but small at the best of times, yet their masters are unable to help them by reason their trading is taken from them, for the merchants will not buy their Bayes so that these stocks lying dead in their hands are hardly able to help themselves...'

Having painted this sorry picture of the state of trade, they went on to hint at the desperation they were nearing:

> '...And had it not been that the right honourable the Earl of Warwick,...and others, worthy gentlemen, had appeased them, many wretched people would have gathered together in a Mutiny...to have made their miseries known to your Majesty, for they said words would not fill the belly nor clothe the back'.

Reason and moderation did not prevail, nor were they likely to, for starving men cannot afford the luxury of such virtues. A fortnight after this plea was sent, a food riot broke out. Hearing no reply to their desperate call, 300 hungry weavers could wait no longer. They gathered from Braintree and Bocking and marched to Maldon, where they raided a ship belonging to two north-country merchants which was carrying corn to Hull. The mob boarded the ship before it could sail and relieved it of as much grain as they could carry. For good measure, they lightened the chief merchant's pocket by £20. They paid dearly for this attempt to appease their own and their families' hunger. Four men were caught; one was later reprieved, but the other three were hanged. A Maldon woman, Agnes Clarke, who described herself as their captain and who, it was alleged, had been touring the distressed areas stirring up revolt, was hanged with them.

Periods of hunger and distress were frequent in cloth towns. This was largely because the trade was at the mercy of communications with its overseas markets in Spain and Portugal. If these broke down, or if heavy import duties were imposed, then the Essex clothiers faced financial disaster and their workers starvation. In 1657 there was a major scare when the Government slapped a high duty on Portuguese and Spanish wines. Fearing reprisals from the governments of Spain and Portugal, the Braintree and Bocking clothiers petitioned Parliament, reminding them in no uncertain terms, that nine-tenths of their bays and says went to Spain and Portugal and that any disruption of their trade with these countries 'would destroy the woollen manufactory of Essex', and would bring ruin to the families of spinners, weavers, and combers—a total of 50-60,000 people.

Despite its ups and downs, the manufacture of cloth in Braintree and Bocking continued to grow. By 1700, the combined output of the twin towns exceeded that of all other Essex towns except Colchester. Yet, within 15 years, there were unmistakable signs of a general, and permanent decline. At the start of the 18th century, the weavers were concentrated in Braintree and Bocking, and some of the nearer villages such as Rayne and Stisted. Spinners were spread further afield, with local clothiers putting out work all over North Essex. In this respect, little had changed since the 14th century. Yet as the century progressed, weavers, and to a lesser degree spinners, became fewer in the rural areas, as decline began to bite.

The list of Braintree bankrupts is a clue to the difficulties most clothiers faced. Throughout the century there were 25 bankrupts, of whom five were clothiers and a further three were 'bay-makers'. The names of their creditors is a reminder that most clothiers bought their wool from sellers of fleeces ('fellmongers') in London:

Braintree Bankrupts

24.11.1720	John Windell, Braintree, bay maker. Creditor, Daniel Legg, London, merchant taylor.
3.2.1738	Thomas Amies, Bocking, woolman and chapman (a pedlar or small merchant).
17.11.1743	Thomas Ruggles, the younger, Bocking clothier.
19.2.1747	Robert Bell, Braintree, clothier.
27.12.1752	John Paine, the elder, Braintree, clothier.
13.1.1753	John Payne, the younger, Braintree, clothier.
1.11.1753	William Peers, Braintree, clothier. Creditors: A. Veernham, T. Hill, and J. Russell, all of Bermondsey, fellmongers; J. Nicholas and M. Papmaen, Southwark, fellmongers.
30.10.1780	Joseph English, Bocking, bay-maker.
11.7.1796	Thomas Lewis, late of Bocking, bay-maker.

John Windell, the first named above, belonged to a family which had been carrying on the cloth trade in Braintree for well over a century. The trade was no respecter of tradition, though, and, just as it could make fortunes, it could also lead to penury. At the time of the 1720 slump, Windell employed 23 weavers, and according to one estimate, about 120 spinners. His stock and equipment were valued at approximately £1,100, and his premises comprised at least 13 different departments for storing and processing the cloth at its various stages of production. There were no spinning wheels or looms amongst his equipment, an indication that these were owned and kept by the spinners and weavers themselves. Like most clothiers in the town, Windell was a prominent citizen and was even a member of the '4 & 20'. That such a man could be brought to ruin by the vagaries of the cloth trade indicates the precariousness of the town's economic position.

The Nottage family of 'Fulling Mill House' ran one of the largest businesses in Bradford Street. Like so many clothiers, they were Huguenot refugees who had fled France when the Revocation of the Edict of Nantes (1685) made them vulnerable to Catholic persecution. In 1774, Nottidge sent 1,570 pieces of baize to London, a weekly average of about 30 pieces, from which figure it has been estimated that he employed around 50 weavers, and up to 500 spinners. The fluctuation of trade is revealed by the variation in his annual output from around 750 pieces in a poor year to nearly 3,000 in a good one. For the period 1775-86 his average was 1,730 annually, but from then on his operations dwindled fast until in December 1789 he wrote 'Sent 9 bays. These are my last'.

A vivid glimpse of the last 100 years of the cloth trade in Braintree and Bocking is provided in the pages of a diary kept by two members of the Savill family. Joseph Savill (1721-88) and his son John (1753-1828) ran one of the largest businesses in Bocking until 1819 when, as the last remaining clothier in the two parishes, John sold his Bocking Church Street mill to the silk manufacturer Samuel Courtauld. At the peak of their business they owned two water-mills—one at Bocking, the other Bulford Mill, Black Notley—extensive premises for storing wool and finished cloth, and a carrier's business for transporting their cloth to London.

The diary and correspondence of these two puts flesh on the bare bones of an account of a clothier's life. We learn, for example, of the interest Joseph Savill showed in his overseas markets. He was, quite naturally, concerned about the state of trade in Portugal and wished to be kept in close touch. In May, 1743 he received a letter from Thomas Sayer (possibly his agent) describing Lisbon:

> 'Full of fruit trees that you should be amazed to see them. There is also an abundance of Game in the country which are free for anyone...wine we have in abundance for which in the tavern we pay about 3d a bottle. Everything is very agreeable and pleasant but its very hot...I like it very well but miss the Brayntry Beer which if you are ketched with any liquor but what is the country's produce you are sent to prison.
>
> I am yours at command,
>
> Thomas Sayer

Events in Lisbon were worthy of an entry in the diary, for they often had a direct effect on the business:

> November 1st, 1755
>
> 'Earthquake at Lisbon...which entirely destroyed the city and put such a stop to our trade that we rise from six Notts a penny Woof to eight in one day. Most of our merchants meet with such losses as we are afraid will ruin them.'

The 1750s were a difficult time, both in the local cloth trade and for the town itself. A spate of robberies and a case of incendiarism were signs of poverty and discontent.

Joseph Savill noted these in his diary, and commented upon them with growing alarm. As a wealthy clothier, he was a prime target for robbers and, to add to his worries, the decade ended with a strike—a desperate measure at the time—among his weavers.

> 'May, 1757. Benjamin Howard's waggon was stopped at Braintree as it was going to Maldon with 7 Quarters and ½ of wheat by a mobb of women and they took away 7 sacks of it to their own use and the same day Mr Baines' waggon was stopped in Church Street, Bocking by a mobb of women who made him unload and sell ye wheat in the street at 5 shillings per bushell.
> May, 1757. Samuel Ruggles Barn in Church Lane was sett on fire and burnt down with 20 acres of Corn and 50 packs of wool. Almost £300 of damage done.
> November, 1758. The weavers and tradesmen differed about bringing home the waste. The Master insisted upon ye Waste and the weavers would not bring it home and so they went off weaving and went to Camp.'

The dispute over who was to bring in the waste wool was a drawn-out affair. By January 1759 Savill was at a low ebb, as was his trade. He had not sold a single Bay in the entire year and now had a stock of 726 'long Bays' in his barn. The weavers stayed out for 14 weeks—a considerable achievement for the winter when no temporary farm work was available. The strain was beginning to tell on Savill. In April of that year, he writes 'weighed myself and I weigh 9 stone just'. Moreover, as if to prove the saying that troubles never come singly, in September he was conscripted into the Militia. But wealth cushioned him against this misfortune, and he was able to pay a certain Daniel Taylor 47 shillings to serve in his place. To complete his run of bad luck an entry for the following week records: 'Bought two lottery tickets at £11 5s 0d each. Both blanks'. Even the weather seemed to conspire against him in this month of misfortune:

> 'Very high wind as ever i knowed blew. Thomas Livermore's 2 chimneys down and 2 apple trees and blew down Aunt Larkins' Chimneys down at ye Woolpack and did a great deal of damage in town'.

The early 1760s brought an improvement in trade, and in 1763 Savill made a clear profit of £1,000. But the next downturn was always just around the corner in this unstable trade and by 1767 he was making a loss of over £300. Even in good times, the benefits of the trade did not always reach the weavers themselves. In 1772—a good year for trade—Savill notes 'the Mobb was up in all ye towns around about on account of provisions being so dear'. They 'stopped the waggons with corn and meat and sold as they pleased and whent to farm houses and collected money and some places took ye corn and made the farmer bring it to town and sell it at these prices: Wheat 7s a bushell; Barley 3s 6d; Beef 4½ d a lb.; Veal 5d; Mutton 5d; Pork 5d; Cheese 5d; Butter 8d...'. Astonishingly, these prices were quite high by comparison with the average for the time. This suggests that prices had risen to a seasonal high beyond the reach of the poor.

The last quarter of the 18th century saw a steady decline in the cloth trade, and gloom descended as war brought confusion to the trade routes:

> 'Spinners not half work to do what with America and Spain and French war with us and a very alarming mob in London about the Roman Catholick Bill. I think I never looked upon our national affairs in so gloomy a light. I have now unsold more than 1,050 Bays and no prospect of selling. Wool never cheaper and trade never worse.'

Joseph Savill died in 1788 and his son John succeeded to the business. While the elder Savill had seen the cloth trade go from prosperity into decline, the younger witnessed the painfully slow death of the industry and its replacement by the factory-based manufacture of silk.

John Savill held out bravely against the end of the industry, until he was the last remaining clothier in the Braintree and Bocking area. Although his personal wealth was assured by his income from his by now large farming interests, he tried to keep the industry going largely to provide work for the under-employed weavers in the town. He pinned his hopes on the introduction of mechanisation and the production of new types of cloth. His willingness to learn from the much newer textile industry of the North of England took him on a tour of the textile towns there. With another Bocking clothier, Josiah Nottidge, he rode around 'to gain what information we could in the mode of manufacturing by machinery and to procure some for ourselves which we did'. This was in December 1801, and by June he was able to record in the diary: 'John Jubb came from Leeds to put up my carding and spinning machinery'. Within three weeks he had 'sett the machines to work'.

Savill also experimented with new products. In 1800 he was making blankets at the rate of 500 a year. He served the prosperous farmers with horse-cloths, horse-rugs, and collar-cloth. He financed a hemp-making business to provide work for out-of-work weavers. But all his ingenuity was not enough to save the cloth trade when the Napoleonic War (1803-15) delivered the final blow. Such a long period of disruption to trade could not be borne even by Savill. Although he did continue to make bays for a short time after the return of peace, he finally made the decision to sell the Bocking Church Street water-mill to the silk manufacturer, Samuel Courtauld, in 1819.

The Savills' diary hints at some of the causes of the industry's decline. Most serious was the over-reliance on the Portuguese market. Whenever communications were broken, the English cloth industry lost trade and contracts to its main competitor, France. On the other hand, John Savill's use of machinery belies the allegation which has been made of Essex clothiers that they were slow to introduce new methods of production. A more valid cause was the hostility of the weavers to labour-saving machinery. The burning of Samuel Ruggles' barn, mentioned earlier, was probably a reaction to his installation of a wool-mill. This device cleaned and loosened the wool and almost halved labour costs. The determination of Essex weavers to fight for their jobs may have been one of the attractions of the North of England, where there was no tradition of labour troubles. The Essex weavers were relatively militant for the time. A society of Braintree weavers may well have been behind the strike at Savill's in 1758-59. A few years earlier the Braintree workers had formed a co-operative to buy flour in bulk for sale to members, and this may have provided the funds to support the 14 week strike. In the end, though, the workers were as helpless as the clothiers in the face of larger forces, and the industry died. There was one difference, while the clothier could fall back on his farms and rents, the weaver, with his redundant skills, faced starvation or the workhouse.

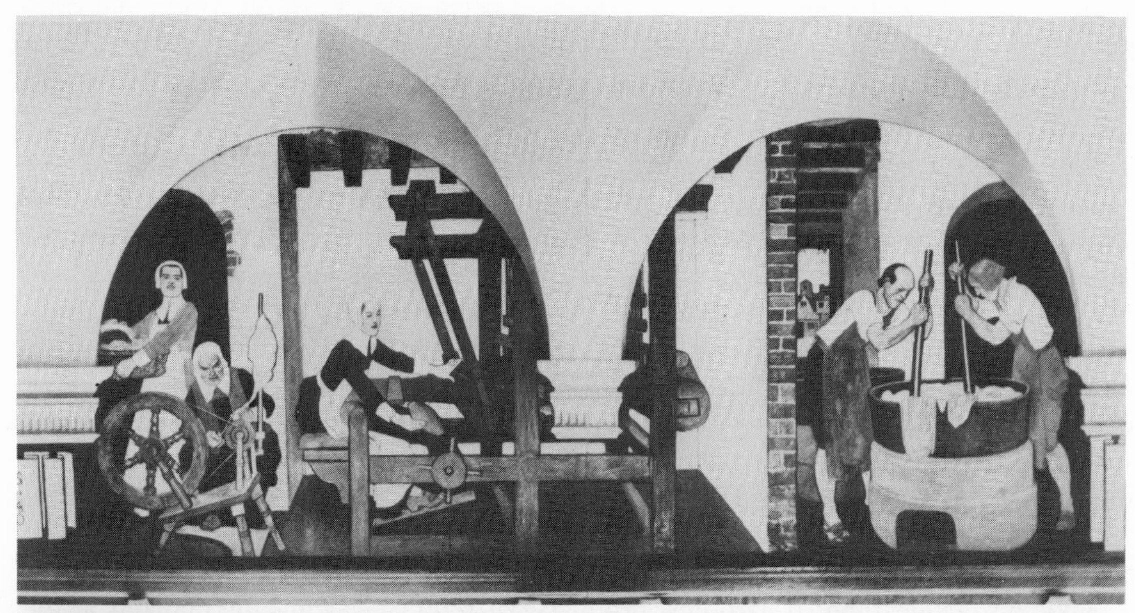

ABOVE: Huguenots spinning, weaving and dyeing, c1690. From Town Hall Murals. (ERO/JA) BELOW: Bradford Street from the junction with Courtauld Road, c1900. (ERO/JA)

ABOVE: Sketch of 'Bocking Street', now Bradford Street, 1889. (ERO/JA)
BELOW: Bradford Street, c1900. (NG)

ABOVE: Mr & Mrs Nottage of Bocking. (ERO/JA) BELOW: Convent and Fulling Mill House, former home of the Nottage family. (ERO/JA)

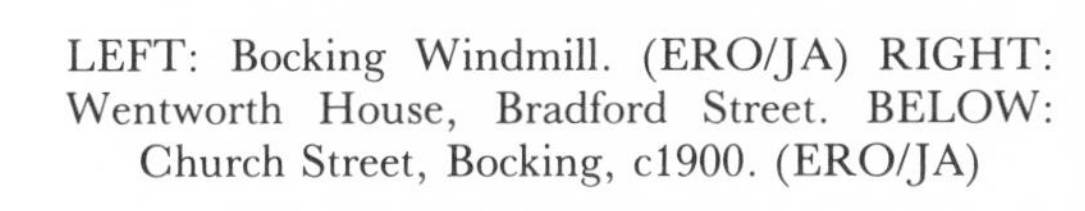

LEFT: Bocking Windmill. (ERO/JA) RIGHT: Wentworth House, Bradford Street. BELOW: Church Street, Bocking, c1900. (ERO/JA)

ABOVE: Savill family tomb, Bocking End Congregational Church. CENTRE: The Causeway, Bocking End. (ERO/JA) BELOW: Braintree Museum, Bradford Street.

ABOVE: The Green at Bocking, c1890. (ERO/JA) BELOW: Redclyffe, Bocking End, c1890. (ERO/JA)

ABOVE: Courtauld's Braintree Mill, Chapel Hill entrance, c1900. (ERO/JA) BELOW: The Great Fire at the Braintree Mill, 9 December, 1909. (ERO/JA)

Those Magnificent Mills

The story of Braintree's silk industry, which replaced the dying cloth trade and eased the town into the industrial age, begins on a small island just off the west coast of France. For it was from the island of Oléron that Augustin Courtauld set out for England in the 17th century. Like thousands of other Protestants he was driven out of his country by religious persecution. When the Revocation of the Edict of Nantes (1685) ended the religious freedoms which the French Protestant Huguenots had been permitted, some 200,000 of them emigrated. The arrival of many of them in England was a great stimulus to commercial and industrial life.

Augustin Courtauld was followed, a few years later, by his son, thereby establishing the main line of the Courtauld family on English soil. Throughout the 18th century the family were working goldsmiths in London. George Courtauld, the great-grandson of Augustin, was the first to break this tradition when, at the age of 14, he was apprenticed to a silk-throwster of Spitalfields in 1775. After he had served his seven-year apprenticeship, George set up on his own as a throwster. In time he became a manager for a Spitalfields firm and set up a water-powered silk mill for them at Pebmarsh, just 12 miles from Braintree. This was in 1799, and soon after he began to look around for another water-mill to run himself.

By 1809 he had achieved his aim. With a partner named Wilson, he took joint-ownership of an old flour mill which stood at the foot of Chapel Hill in Braintree. He immediately set about converting it into a working silk mill. The old premises were largely demolished and replaced by a larger building with a deeper mill-race and a bigger water-wheel. By 1810, on the spot where water had powered the grinding of corn since before Domesday, a wheel was driving machines for the throwing and weaving of silk.

The raw silk for the mill—mostly Italian, Chinese and Bengali— was sent by carrier from London to Braintree. Here it was woven into a 'hard silk' and subjected to various dressings and finished until it became a stiff, and usually black, fabric. This was Crape, the material which later in the century was to make a fortune for the Courtaulds. This first Braintree mill, however, soon ran into trouble when the partners quarrelled. After legal proceedings, Wilson kept the mill and George received compensation and agreed not to take any part in the manufacturing of silk within ten miles of Braintree before April 1829.

Despite this failure, the seed of the Courtauld business in Braintree had been sown.

One of the workers at this first mill had been George's son, Samuel Courtauld III. He too fell out with his apparently irascible father and left home at the age of 18 in 1811 or 1812. Four years later he returned to Braintree and set up as a silk throwster in a small building in Panfield Lane. It was an immediate success. By 1818 he was doing well enough to build 'a factory for horse power large enough to about treble our business'. He paid £120 for the site which lay on the north side of South Street, known as Pound End. This land had formed part of the garden to the house of William Grant, the infamous Braintree miser, which stood in New Street.

By April of that year the building was complete and the machines were set to work in May. However, almost as quickly as it had begun, the venture ran into trouble. The first year was so disastrous that Samuel began searching for a water-powered mill. He finally secured a lease, with the option to buy, on Savill's cloth-fulling mill in Bocking. So, in November 1819, he transferred his business from the ill-fated Pound End Mill to Bocking. The fine, weather-boarded mill in South Street, though it was never again used by Courtaulds, was later to house several important Braintree businesses, namely the silk firms Walters and Warners, and the engineering works of Joseph Bradbury. Although Samuel Courtauld operated the mill for only six months, it continued to be known, down to this century, as 'Courtauld's Old Factory'.

The Bocking mill was a success and soon produced profits of around £1,000 a year. Although still relying on water power, the silk industry benefitted from the legacy of the cloth trade. In particular there was a ready supply of young women and children with textile skills to work in the throwing-mills and a pool of unemployed handloom weavers for silk weaving. The slow death of the cloth trade had kept wages low, and a combination of this and a rising population meant poverty was rife. So, there was a workforce willing and ready to work for two-thirds of the wages paid in Spitalfields.

Samuel Courtauld's business expanded during the 1820s. In 1825 he took over and converted to crape production a water-driven corn-mill at nearby Halstead. The following year he built a steam factory next to Savill's old mill at Bocking, and later added a finishing factory. His new prosperity enabled him to move to the large 'Folly House' at High Garrett, close to his Bocking factory which was clearly becoming the centre of his North-Essex operations. In Braintree, the small Panfield Lane factory was still working until about 1833. Also, handloom weavers in the town were still weaving in their own homes for Courtauld, and for a short time there was a broad silk Warehouse in the High Street.

In 1843, Samuel turned his energies towards Braintree again. In that year he bought the Chapel Hill Mill which his father had originally converted in 1809. This came at about the same time as the firm entered a 35-year period of sustained growth, thanks largely to mid-Victorian Britain's taste for mourning crape. The association between respectability and ostentatious mourning was a great boon to Courtaulds. In 1859, as expansion continued apace, a three-storey mill was built next to the old mill at Chapel Hill. Winding, throwing, and power-weaving were begun, and Braintree's handloom weavers took one step closer to extinction.

The mushroom-like growth of the silk industry in this rural area, particularly after 1850, brought huge changes within the lifetime of many workers. The cloth trade had been organised entirely on the domestic outwork system. By 1850 the weaver working in his own cottage was a thing of the past. Life in a factory was very different and, with Courtauld's near monopoly on employment in the town, it affected a large proportion of the population. By the 1880s, more than 1,300 workers were employed by the firm at Braintree and Bocking, at a time when the combined population was only 8,500. The silk industry also changed the composition of the workforce. In 1833, in East Anglia, 96% of all silk workers were women. More than half of these were under 16, and an astonishing 14% were under 11. The reason for this was simple: women and children were nimble-fingered—essential in the manufacture of silk—and worked for less than adult males.

Another revolutionary change in working life was the introduction of shift work. Samuel Courtauld used a double set of 'hands', each working 12 hours, to keep his mills going day and night. This was just one of the ways in which the factory was driving a wedge between the town and the country. Not only had working conditions for the urban worker become worse, they also became poorer. Although the silk industry had originally paid high wages and provided full employment, this did not last. At the start of the 19th century, silk weavers could earn 12-15s a week. By contrast, agricultural wages were about 10s, plus some extra benefits such as beer or malt and the opportunity to keep a pig or grow vegetables. At this time the standard of living in town and country was roughly equal. But wages in the silk industry fell sharply. By the 1830s, weavers were earning 7-13s a week.

Courtaulds could lower wages in this way because work in the area was in short supply. No-one was going to risk losing their job by complaining. There was no difficulty in finding employees. Workhouse children were a ready source, and regulations restricting the working hours of women and children had little effect in the silk industry until mid-century. Even after the Ten Hours Act (1847), women and children were still working a 60 hour week. Courtaulds were unwilling to lose their child workforce, whom they could pay far less than adults. The 19th century Factory Acts chipped away at the exploitation of child labour, but progress was slow. Real improvement came only late in the century with the realisation that the nation's industry would be better served by a workforce able to read and write.

It is unfair to paint too black a picture of Samuel Courtauld. He was not a demon in charge of a 'satanic mill'. Although he would tolerate no form of trade union activity, he showed a paternalistic regard for the welfare of his workers. He instituted a system of rewards and punishments for his workforce, offering beer as an inducement to hard work and fines, corporal punishment, and dunce's hats as punishment for slackers. He and other members of the family built schools, reading rooms and workers' cottages in Braintree and surrounding towns. George Courtauld II donated £2,000 to build the Manor Street School in 1862 and a further endowment for the Braintree and Bocking Literary and Mechanics Institute at Bocking End. The full list of the family's gifts to the area is a long one, and it continues well into the present century.

The silk industry brought enormous wealth to the Courtauld family. In 1854 Samuel bought Gosfield Hall for £33,400, a vast sum at a time when a cottage could be built for about £500. He eventually became a landowner to the extent of 3,200 acres. The phenomenon of the wealthy industrialist was new to Essex, and that Samuel Courtauld, silk manufacturer, should follow the Earl of Nugent and the Marquises of Buckingham as owner of the Hall, must have been a bitter pill for the 'county set' to swallow. Indeed he never became a part of that set, nor, probably, did he wish to. For he was a self-made man, and proud of it, whose politics differed greatly from those of the Tory gentry. His espousal of Liberal-Radical politics, his active campaigning for political reform, and his leadership in the Dissenters' cause during the famous Braintree Church Rate Case, all combined to make him a sharp thorn in the Tory-Anglican establishment's side. Furthermore, his quirky character—he was autocratic, dominant, and tended to paranoia—was not the best asset in the world of polite intercourse. He died in 1881, aged 87, having amassed a fortune of £700,000 and become a virtual recluse in his huge mansion set in the privacy of its parkland.

The influence of the Courtaulds on Braintree is significant. Without the silk industry the town would have developed in very different ways during the 19th century, and the end of the cloth trade would have been an even more serious blow to the town's prosperity. Once Courtaulds were established, they attracted other silk firms to the town. In one case, Courtaulds built the mill which provided the start in Braintree for a firm which rose to the same level of international esteem as themselves. This was Walters & Sons, who were later taken over by Warner & Sons.

After Samuel Courtauld had moved his machinery to Bocking in 1819, the Pound End Mill stood empty, only months after its opening. By 1822, though, it was being leased by Daniel Walters, a silk manufacturer, for £65 a year. Walters was the son of a Spitalfields silk weaver who had taken over his father's business. Around 1820, like several Spitalfields silk manufacturers, he had moved out of London, where a fixed wage-rate among weavers was cutting into profits. Like the Courtaulds, he found the conditions at Braintree attractive and chose the town as the new home for his silk factory. Walters' aim was to make high quality goods. In this he was joined by a few of the more far-sighted silk manufacturers who wanted to raise British silk weaving beyond the standards of Continental manufacture. This paid off when, in 1860, the duties on French silks were removed as part of a treaty with France. Without protection, the British silk industry was dealt a blow which was fatal to all but those firms able to compete on equal terms.

Walters soon built up a reputation for fine silks and velvets, chiefly for use as furniture covers. Around 1840, they moved into figured fabrics rather than plains. Nine years later, by which time they were recognised as one of the chief makers of furniture silks in the country, they won the Gold Isis Medal of the Royal Society of Arts. In 1861 the *People's History of Essex* stated: 'The firm employs 150 jacquard machines and nearly 300 hands, and is one of the foremost in the kingdom for superiority of design and beauty of workmanship...The house has a good foreign trade, and the very richest brocatelle damasks, tissued satins, etc. which adorn the palaces of our Queen are produced in these works at Braintree'. Yet despite this glowing praise, this was a hard year for the silk industry, and neither Walters nor Courtaulds were immune to the crisis of confidence which beset silk manufacturers. For Braintree, with its hopes pinned on the success of silk, it was a worrying time.

In June a public meeting was called in response to the distress among weavers which was said to be greater than ever before. Yet Walters gambled by building a new factory. This act of faith in their ability to win through by the high standard of their product paid off. The opening of the factory was an occasion for celebration among weavers who, just two months earlier had been told there was no prospect of employment. A newspaper account of that August opening was couched in euphoric terms; the confidence booster had worked: 'The workpeople assembled at the old factory, whence, headed by a brass band, they walked in procession, bearing a variety of beautiful banners, specimens of their workmanship, through the town to the new building. Here they partook of an excellent dinner...and the festivities were kept up by a Ball in the evening'.

The new mill, a two-storey building, was built just over the parish boundary in Black Notley, which at that time reached within the town limits. About 1869 or 1870 it was moved across the Brain valley to the south of Pound End to form part of the complex known as 'New Mills'. Sited on the south side of South Street this group of buildings was finished in 1877 and consisted of two long weaving sheds, one shorter one, a dyehouse and a workshop. These buildings housed the businesses of both Walters and Warners until weaving stopped nearly a century later in 1971.

Walters was a man in the Courtauld mould. He reduced the wages of his weavers and, on one occasion, imposed a 'lock-out' when they complained. But he also laid on an annual beanfeast for his employees. The following is a newspaper account of one of these happy occasions in 1867: 'On Friday last, the employees of Messrs Walters & Sons, had their annual outing. A special train was engaged to leave Braintree at an early hour for Walton-on-the-Naze, prior to which the hands, numbering with their friends nearly 400, and accompanied by the band of the 12th Essex Rifles, paraded the principal streets of the town and marched to the railway station.

'Arriving at Walton, a substantial breakfast was taken at the Clifton Hotel and the visitors then dispersed to amuse themselves as they thought best. Upon again arriving at Braintree, a procession was formed and, preceded by a lively display of coloured fire, marched into town, everyone appearing well pleased with the holiday he had enjoyed.'

Daniel Walters was slow to introduce steam power. Unlike Courtaulds, who had built a steam factory—probably the first in the Essex silk industry—next to Savill's old mill at Bocking in 1826, Walters did not use power looms until 1870. In that year a talented engineer named Bradbury (the founder of the engineering firm) came from the north of England to run the new looms. An ingenious and inventive man,

Bradbury designed and built himself new equipment including looms and jacquards (apparatus for weaving figured fabrics).

Courtaulds and Walters, who were taken over by Warner & Sons in 1895, survived longer than any other Essex silk businesses. Yet each survived for very different reasons. Courtaulds began to diversify early. They were one of the first to produce black mourning Crape, and profited hugely when this became fashionable. Production increased tenfold from 1830 to 1850, and thereafter it became the firm's main product. Also vital to their survival, was the speed with which they experimented with new machinery and production techniques, so giving themselves a competitive edge over their rivals. Walters, by contrast, succeeded through specialisation in luxury fabrics and by continuing to use time-honoured methods of production geared to quality, not quantity.

Several other silk firms operated in Braintree, but they were mostly short-lived compared with the big two. The factories were largely concentrated just off the High Street, in Factory Yard and Martin's Yard. The silk workers lived close to the factories in these narrow, tightly-packed clusters of buildings. The 1851 Census gives a glimpse of the way these small communities were dominated by the silk factory. Living in the 14 cramped cottages in Martin's Yard were no less than 19 silk workers. One of these families had moved to the town from Spitalfields earlier in the year. Head of the household was Thomas Owen, a 61-year-old hand-loom weaver. He, like the other hand-loom weavers in the Yard, was probably a domestic worker, while his wife, a silk winder, probably worked in the factory. The whole Yard was like a sprawling factory, with winding and throwing in the factory shed, and weaving being done in the weavers' cottages. Homes like these can still be seen in St Michael's Road, just opposite the church. Most have three storeys, with the looms originally on the middle floor, between the living quarters and the bedrooms.

The group of small factories around the junction of High Street-London Road-St Michael's Road created a distinctive working-class neighbourhood during the 19th century. Scarcely anywhere else in the town was one group of workers so closely crowded together. They were among the poorest people in the town. Several of the households were headed by women who, while trying to bring up young families, both worked in the silk factories and took in lodgers. For example, one of the Martin's Yard cottages was occupied by: Hannah Frost, householder, widow, and silk warper, aged 42; her daughter, Elizabeth, a silk winder, aged 19; her son, James, a schoolboy, aged 11; her daughter, Hannah, a schoolgirl, aged 8; Sarah Smith, a lodger, unmarried, who worked as a silk winder, and her 9 year-old daughter; and Susannah Cutts, lodger, also a silk winder.

Life for the families in these silk factory yards was closer to that in the northern towns of the early industrial age than that in a rural market town. A large number of the inhabitants were immigrants—mostly from nearby Essex villages or from towns on the Essex-Suffolk border—and a disproportionate number were young, frequently teenage, working girls. The factory dominated their lives—10-12 hours of each day, six days a week, were spent there, and the rest was spent within sight and sound of the factory, in slum-dwellings packed with their fellow workpeople.

Towards the end of the century, the hard times of the workers spread to the manufacturers. One by one they went out of business, with only the two largest firms surviving into the present century. Changes in fashion, in particular the decline of the Victorian penchant for mourning crape, brought a slump in trade for both firms in the 1880s and '90s. Courtaulds were big enough to ride the depression, but Walters went into liquidation in 1894. The prospect for Braintree's weavers was bleak. So it was with great relief that the townspeople welcomed the news, in May 1895, that Benjamin Warner, a London silk manufacturer, was to take over Walters' New Mills.

Many weavers who had left Braintree for London the year before returned, and several London weavers came with them. A few of the latter were true city-dwellers who had never been this far from the capital before. Their mates, so the story goes, had told them to take the tram at Braintree station to the silk mills. A few found it too desolate and quiet and returned to London. In time though, the firm moved all their weaving to Braintree and closed their London factory.

Almost from the start, the power looms were laid aside, and later broken up. Frank Warner took responsibility for production and it was his influence which led to the firm's emphasis on quality silks. According to Warners' historian, Alec Hunter, he was single-minded in his love of the craft which he had learnt from his father and during a spell in the French silk centre of Lyons. He made many experiments, particularly in the weaving of figured velvets, and won Royal orders for the firm. Among these were the Coronation Robes for King Edward VII. This prestigious event was described in the *Essex County Chronicle* for March 1902: 'The weaving of the sumptuouscloth of gold for the vestments to be worn by the King and Queen at the Coronation on June 26th has been completed at Messrs Warners' Silk Works, Braintree. During the few weeks that the cloth of gold and the Royal purple have been in the course of manufacture, many hundreds of visitors have visited the factory and admired these valuable fabrics as they have been produced on quaint old-fashioned handlooms'.

Power-weaving was eventually reintroduced in 1918, and furniture fabrics became the chief product. Yet at each Coronation the hand-looms were called upon. The last of these Royal orders were for Queen Elizabeth II's Coronation in 1953 and for the Investiture of the Prince of Wales in 1969. Sadly, in 1971, 'steeply rising costs' and the contraction of the market for their high quality expensive goods forced the firm to stop weaving, bringing to an end an almost unbroken occupation of the site by the two silk firms which had lasted for over 150 years.

Courtaulds pulled themselves out of the late 19th century depression in a very different way. After a moderate success based on diversification of products after 1899, the real breakthrough came with the replacement of silk by the new man-made fibres. In 1904, the firm bought the British rights to the 'viscose' process of making rayon, invented by British chemists, and developed the world's first commercially successful man-made fibre. Braintree's textile industry was about to enter a new age—one far removed from the hand-loom weaving of silk. Other changes came too. Essex labour was short, so the firm recruited from the northern textile centres, and with this came a bitter pill for the paternalistic firm: the trade union. A branch of the East Riding of Yorkshire Weavers and Textile Workers' Association was formed in 1897 and, the following year, there was a strike at the firm's factory in nearby Halstead. A 'lock-out' by the firm soon won the dispute. But it was a sign of new relations between master and men; the company, and the town , had been firmly shoved into the 20th century.

Braintree Mill gutted by fire. (ERO/JA)

ABOVE: Courtauld's Bocking Mill; (DAB) LEFT, RIGHT and BELOW:
Flooding at Courtauld's Bocking Mill, c1950. (HW)

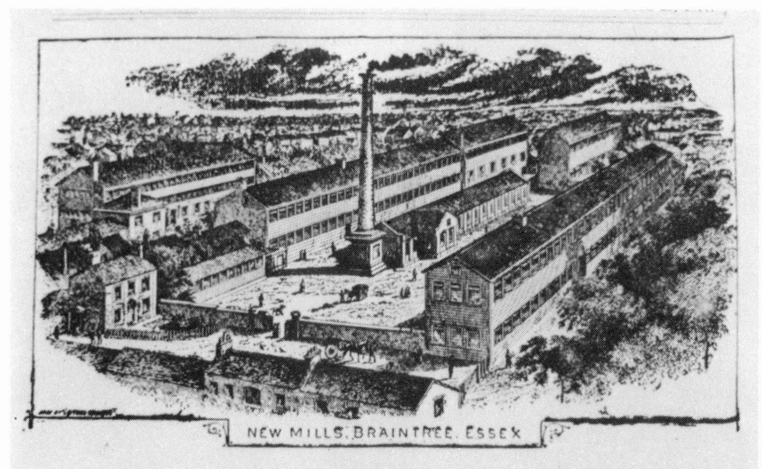

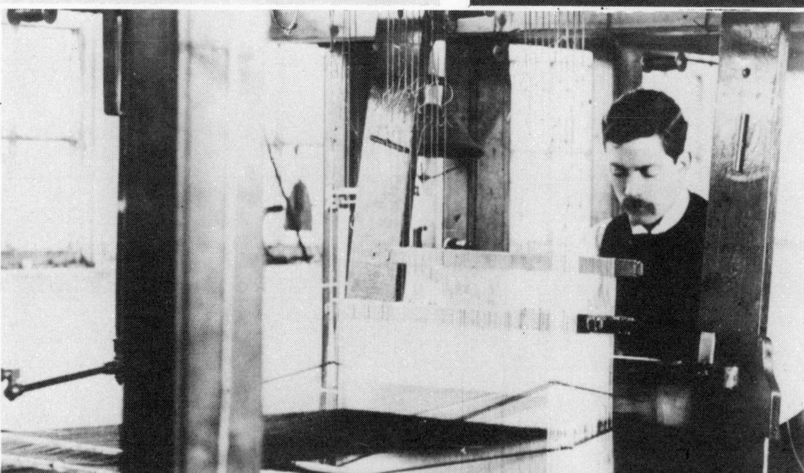

LEFT: Advertisement for Daniel Walters & Sons, 1877. (WA) RIGHT: Benjamin Warner (1828-1908). (WA) CENTRE LEFT: Frank Warner (1862-1930). (WA) RIGHT: Albert Parchment weaving cloth of gold for King Edward VII's Coronation of 1902, at Warner's New Mills. (WA) BELOW: Warner & Sons annual outing, c1898. (WA)

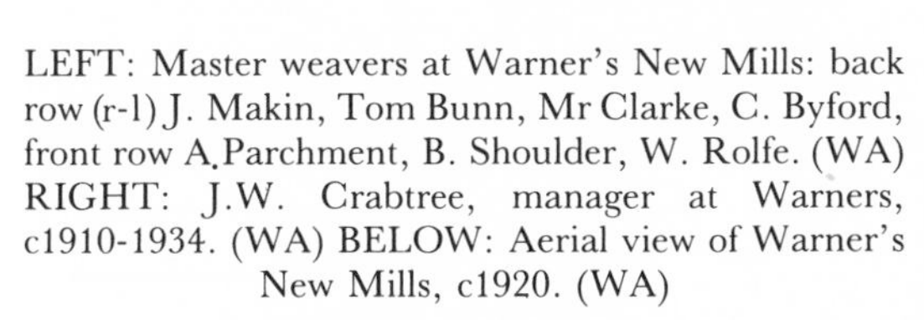

LEFT: Master weavers at Warner's New Mills: back row (r-l) J. Makin, Tom Bunn, Mr Clarke, C. Byford, front row A.Parchment, B. Shoulder, W. Rolfe. (WA) RIGHT: J.W. Crabtree, manager at Warners, c1910-1934. (WA) BELOW: Aerial view of Warner's New Mills, c1920. (WA)

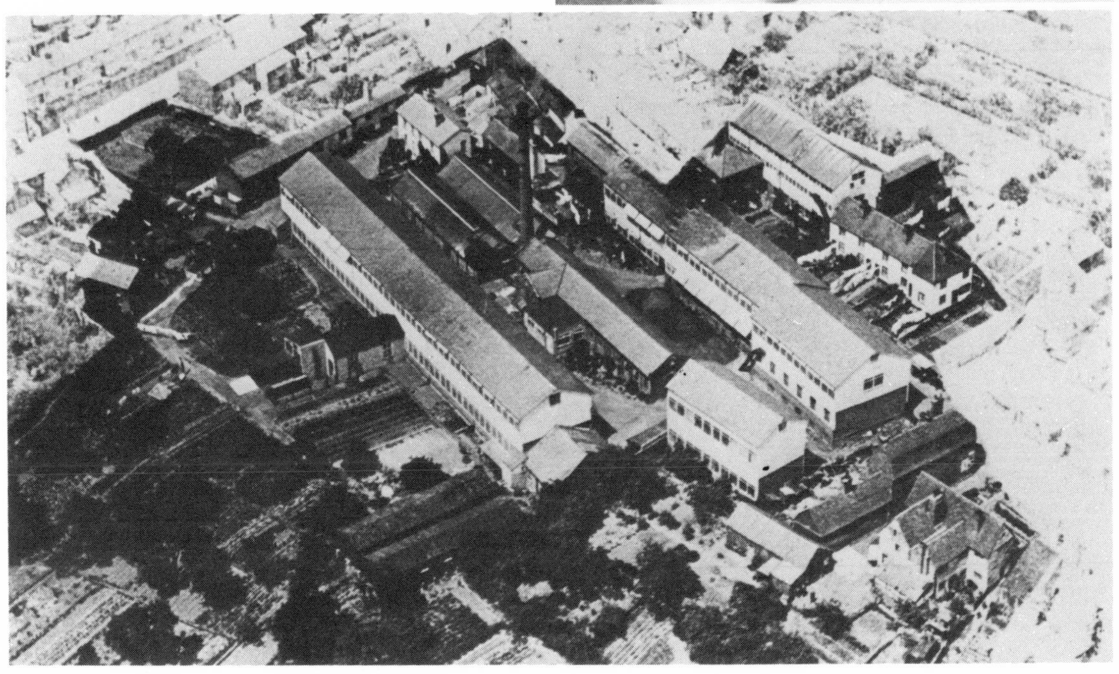

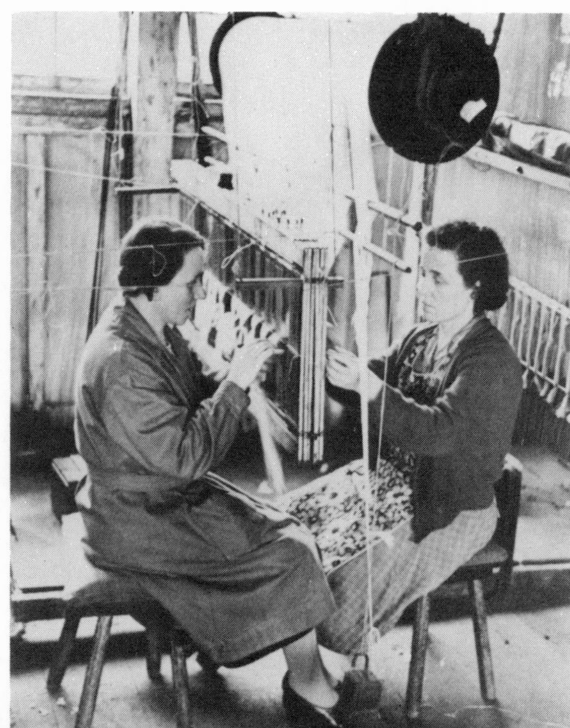

LEFT: Sign outside New Mills, made c1920. (WA) RIGHT: Gladys Watson and Olive Richardson entering up a harness, c1948. (WA) BELOW: Pirn winding, c1937. (WA)

Bert Amos making a warp, c1948. (WA)

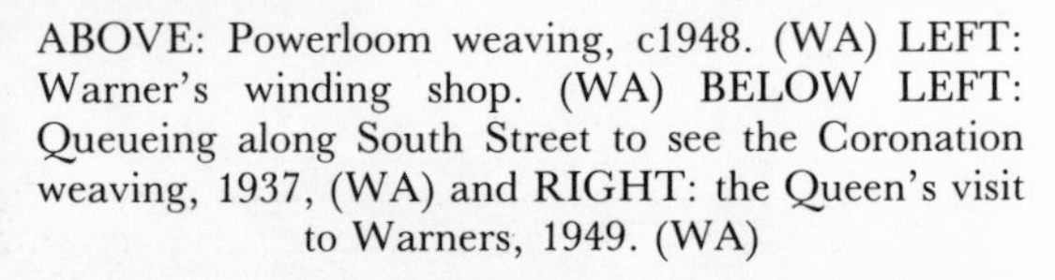

ABOVE: Powerloom weaving, c1948. (WA) LEFT: Warner's winding shop. (WA) BELOW LEFT: Queueing along South Street to see the Coronation weaving, 1937, (WA) and RIGHT: the Queen's visit to Warners, 1949. (WA)

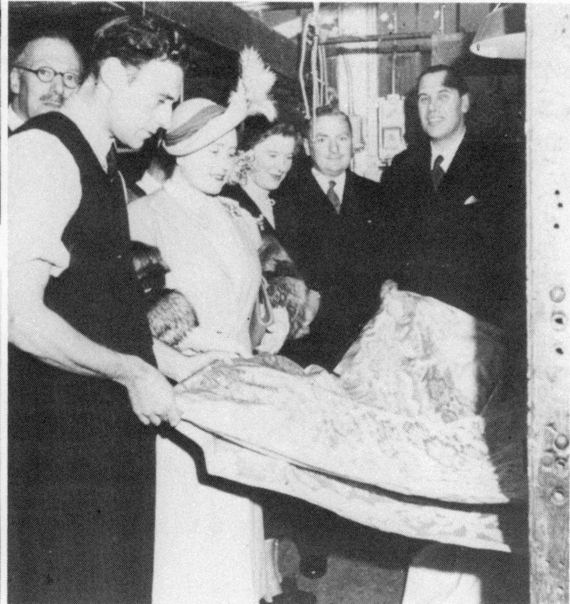

Shades of Poverty

The mixed fortunes of the cloth and silk trades meant that the shadow of poverty was never completely lifted from the town. When the cloth trade finally collapsed towards the end of the 18th century, the Braintree-Bocking area was one of the poorest in the county. It was not only the weavers who suffered; shopkeepers and craftsmen also felt the effects as trade fell off. The problem was a growing one, yet the way of dealing with it had scarcely changed since the Elizabethan period.

The 'Four & Twenty' had borne the responsibility of relieving the poor during the 17th century, but as we have seen they had disappeared by the early 18th century. However a Select Vestry of sorts had taken over the role of guardians of the poor and, by levying a poor-rate, they did their best to provide some relief. In 1720, they appointed a 'Workhouse Committee' to run the parish workhouse. Here the old, sick, and disabled were given what was known a 'indoor-relief' or, in other words, a permanent home in the workhouse. Sometimes the sick and elderly were allowed to stay in their own homes, where they were provided with food, firewood, and had their rents paid.

But the real problem was the growing number of able-bodied, but unemployed men and women. The existing poor laws ordered that no help was to be given to the fit and well except in return for work. Many parishes, including Braintree, ignored this law because of the difficulty of finding and supervising employment. When work for the poor was found it was 'sometimes the manufacture of Hemp-Ware; sometimes to a small extent on the roads; picking, carding, and spinning wool; and occasionally grinding Beans and Malt'. More often than not, though, it was easier for the parish to simply give money, food, and clothing without first demanding work.

Until the 1830s, when there was a major change in the poor laws, the inmates of the Braintree workhouse were mostly the old, the sick and disabled, and the 'weak in mind'. The workhouse stood in the Hyde—now Market Street—roughly on the site now engulfed by Tesco's supermarket. There was room for 60 inmates and the day to day running was left to a workhouse master appointed by the Select Vestry. All inmates were expected to work at a daily task, mostly spinning and carding wool, chopping wood, pumping water, and other small chores. The Workhouse Committee decided the diet of the paupers. For example, in the Committee's minutes for January 1721, we read: 'Ordered that 60lbs of Beef be allowed this week for Thursday, Sunday, and Tuesday. Pease for Wednesday and Friday; that those who will not eat pease have only cheese, and that for breakfast they have either meat-broth, or Pease-Soup, except any be sick then Water-gruel'. Clothing too was provided by the Committee and a typical entry reads: 'William Coleman, a hatt; Isaac Clarke, a shirt and a pair of stockings and mending his shoes; Susan Handly, a pair of pattens (thick wooden clogs); Martha Clay, a pair of shoes and her cote mending; Robert Reeve, a pair of breeches'. Sometimes, so it would seem, these orders were made none too soon as the following indicates: 'Phillip Sly, William Jacob, and Robert Reeve each a waste-cote in order to prevent vermins increase'.

This raises the matter of how sanitary it was in the workhouse. There is no evidence to show that it was particularly bad, as was the case in many parishes, although in September and October of 1721 the inmates were ravaged by a smallpox epidemic. Within a week five were on the sick list and, although the Committee provided a nurse and extra coal for the fire, three eventually died. The general picture is a healthy one—with soap and fruit appearing on the provisions list—especially when compared with the usual diet of the labouring classes which consisted mainly of bread, potatoes, and beer.

The parish workhouse, then, seems to have been run with a firm but humane hand by the Select Vestry. But changes were on the way, both locally and nationally, which were eventually to lead to a new, and harsher, solution to poverty. In Braintree, the population continued to grow and the cloth trade continued its decline. In 1833, the cost of poor relief per head of the population was 18s 2d in Braintree, and 18s 6d in Bocking. By contrast, at Chelmsford it was 6s 6d, and at Saffron Walden only 4s 10d. In response to a country-wide problem, Parliament passed the Poor Law Act of 1834. The new Poor Law made two fundamental changes: it formed several parishes into 'Unions' of parishes to administer poor relief, and ruled that the poor could only be given relief inside the workhouse. The premise was that the poor were poor simply because they were lazy and that if the workhouse was unpleasant enough they would find work rather than apply for relief. It took little account of the fact that in a town like Braintree, where an industry was decaying, there was no work available.

The Braintree Union was declared on 6 December 1835, on which day the Board of Guardians took over the responsibilities of the Select Vestries in the constituent parishes. Two days later the Guardians held their first meeting at the White Hart Inn, at Bocking. Among those present were the important local landowners Charles Savill Onley (of Stisted Hall), George Nottage (of Fulling Mill House, Bradford Street), Samuel Webb Savill, and the Vicar of Braintree, Rev Bernard Scalé. At first the Guardians rented the parish workhouse in Braintree, but this was only a temporary measure. Even after a corn-grinding mill had been installed to provide work for the inmates, the Guardians still felt the need for a new workhouse where a deterrent regime could be efficiently followed.

By August 1836 a three acre site half a mile from the town on Rayne Road had been bought and advertisements for contractors were placed in *The Times, The Morning Chronicle* and local newspapers. Work began in March 1837, and was finished the following year. It had cost almost £7,000 and could accommodate 300 people. Like many workhouses and prisons built at this time, it was based on a design by Jeremy Bentham, and had a small central building from which three arms radiated, with a house at the front. Later the building was enlarged to hold 400 and several acres of land were added. Pigs were introduced in 1850 to consume the refuse. Although the pigs have gone, the workhouse now forms the central part of St Michael's Hospital, and well within living memory it was used as a 'Spike' for tramps passing through the town.

Once the new workhouse—stark and utilitarian, symbolic of its purpose—was ready, the poor were uprooted from their various parishes and brought to Braintree. At the workhouse, already isolated from their friends and neighbours, they were separated from their families. Husbands were parted from their wives, and mothers from their children. Until the day they left the workhouse they lived totally apart. Each entrant was stripped of his own clothes and made to put on the workhouse uniform. The diary of John Castle, a Coggeshall hand-loom weaver, described his experience on entering the Union Workhouse at Witham: 'The first day after dinner we were ordered to strip and put on the regimentals of the Union, which was composed of a pair of thick leather breeches, leather coat, low shoes, ribbed stockings, and hairy cap with a peak'.

Paupers were expected to work from six in the morning to six at night, with half an hour for breakfast and an hour for dinner. This was usually 'oakum-picking', which involved the unravelling of old ropes. No tools were used and each pauper was expected to unravel 3lbs a day—no easy task, for the rope was frequently knotted and tarred and painful on the fingers. The diet was meagre, the cost of keeping each pauper being fixed at 2s 11d a week in 1841. The usual food was bread, third quality butter, seconds flour, cheese, oatmeal, rice, bacon, and 'Common Black Tea'. At dinner and supper the men were usually given a pint of beer, while the women had beer at dinner and tea at supper. Special allowances of beer, tobacco, and snuff were granted to celebrate Queen Victoria's Coronation (1838) and wedding (1840). A similar relaxation of the rules was allowed at Christmas, as the *Essex County Standard* was scandalised to report: '...at Braintree the inmates had roast-beef and plum pudding, a pint of strong beer for each adult, half a pint to each child; pipes, tobacco, and snuff were also given. Pretty doings at Braintree, truly! Paupers eating plum puddings on Christmas Day! What will this world come to?'

If the Braintree Guardians were not the harshest in the country, they could nevertheless be petty and mean. For example, in 1836, they ordered no cooking on Sundays since this caused 'great inconvenience in preventing the workhouse Governor's family going to church'. Or there is this extraordinary piece of Victorian primness: 'Windows of girls' sleeping room to be painted outside, so as to prevent *them* looking into the boys' yard'. Yet, on occasions they stood out against the severity of the Poor Law Commission. They petitioned Parliament in protest against the separation of children from their parents and, in 1842, went so far as to resign en bloc against the ruling of the Commissioners.

There must have been a tale of misery attached to all the inmates. Many were simply old and without a family to turn to. Such things as old age pensions were still a lifetime away. George Smee, a sailor, and his charwoman wife, both aged 80, had only a pauper's grave to look forward to. The same was true for James Goldstone (80) and Thomas Allen (70), both woolcombers and survivors of the long defunct wool trade. Sickness may have been the reason for William Digby's presence there. The 40 year-old fishmonger belonged to a family which had carried on that trade from at least as early as 1826—when John Digby was shown 'hollering mackerel' in the 'Braintree Market' print—and continues today. Often whole families were found in the workhouse. Samuel Rankin, an agricultural labourer, was there with his wife and five children. William, John, and Joseph Peacock, aged 12, 9, and 5, were probably orphans. A missing or dead husband was a frequent reason for a woman and her children to be forced to enter the workhouse. Sometimes they were tragically young, like Mary Bacon, aged 20, with her two young children.

The New Poor Law was hated by the poor, but apart from small rebellions there was little they could do to change it. When a group of paupers at the Braintree workhouse refused to work at the corn-grinding mill, they were put on a bread and water diet. This led to more trouble, and two constables from the Metropolitan Police had to be called in to restore order. This was in April 1837, and a month later rebellion boiled over again. The paupers again refused to do their tasks, claiming that they were not getting enough food. They were brought before the magistrates—three of whom were on the Board of Guardians—and sentenced to hard labour in Chelmsford Gaol. One of the offenders, George Reed, was frequently sent back to the prison, saying he would not work until his allowance of bread was increased. Perhaps he had found that conditions were better in the prison than in the workhouse.

Charles Dickens recognised the horror which the workhouse aroused in the poor. In *Our Mutual Friend*, Mrs Higden says of the workhouse: 'Kill me rather than take me there. Throw this child under cart-horses' feet and a loaded wagon, sooner than take him there'. In case this sounds the stuff of fiction rather than life, compare it with these words spoken by Samuel Everard, a Braintree tailor, in the Market Place: '...sooner than I will be torn from my wife's bosom that has yielded consolation to me in all my trials and difficulties, and from the children we love, I will die in the public streets'. His speech was greeted with 'immense cheering'.

Even for those outside the workhouse, Braintree was an unhealthy place. The town was dimly lit, poorly patrolled by Constables, and stank of human refuse. Until the mid-19th century the only reliable source of clean water was the Town Pump, which stood at the north end of New Street. This remained in use until the 1890s, and explains the recess in the street frontage by Joscelyne's shop. There were no sewers either. Instead, the unwary pedestrian could discover the dung-heaps, cesspools, and open trenches dotted around the town, or might bump into the dung-cart at night.

Although the town had grown considerably, the provisions for public health were scarcely any better by the beginning of the 19th century than they had been at the time of the 'Great Plague', when one-third of the people of Braintree had died. The first step towards a modern public health system came with the creation of the Braintree Board of Health in 1850. The first aim of the Board was to lay a water supply and a sewage system–two services which probably did more than anything else to change the quality of life in the town. By 1864 the waterworks was completed and put into operation. This building still stands, between the river and the railway bridge, in Notley Road.

As the century progressed, Braintree became not only cleaner, but also lighter and safer. In 1833 John Cunnington observed that 'the town is respectably lighted and watched; and though this does not extend to paving, most of the inhabitants of the principal streets have paved the footpaths before their own houses'. Until 1830 the Vestry was responsible for the lighting. The result was not overwhelming; just 60 dim and flickering oil lamps providing isolated pools of light.

After 1830 the Vestry handed over to a Lighting Committee, which raised money by a rate on property. Each year the members of the Committee met to deliberate upon the weighty question of when to put the lights on. Their scrupulous attitude would be a credit to energy-saving campaigns of more recent years. Lights were usually allowed from October to March, except when there was a full moon. The lamps were lit for only a few hours, and by 10 o'clock the town was cast into darkness. Some late night roistering did occur, though, on special days. On Fair Days, for example, the town was illuminated until 3 am. No doubt the lamp-lighter grumbled about having to work so late, though maybe he earned a little more than his usual 8s 6d a week during Fair-time. Even after gas replaced oil in the latter half of the century, he was still to be seen doing his rounds at dusk with a taper torch on the end of a pole.

The same Committee was also responsible for fire-fighting. Between 1840 and 1845 the Braintree Lighting and Watching Inspectors bought several fire-engines. These were nothing more than small carts, equipped with a hand-turned pump, which were pulled to the fire by the firemen themselves. Nevertheless they were a more effective means of fire-fighting than anything that had gone before. The forerunners of the modern police were also appointed by this versatile committee. In the 1830s there were two watchmen who were paid 14s a week to keep an eye on the town in much the same way as the Constables had done in the 16th century.

It is difficult to know the extent of crime in Braintree, but the age-old practices of pick-pocketing, house-breaking, drunkenness, and brawling were still as common in the 19th century as they had ever been. The market had always brought disorder to the town, and rowdy customers to the public houses. An example of this is graphically provided by the account of a brawl between two townsmen in 1745. Robert Butcher alleged that John Firmin had come up to him in the 'Publick Market in Braintree and struck him across the head with a large stick...and afterwards had taken him by the nose and led him by it for several yards'. This, though, was but one of several episodes in the saga of Firmin's animosity towards Butcher.

To start with Firmin had assaulted him in 'the Common Kitchen of Moses Peers, being a public house in Coggeshall Lane' and had 'broke the pipe in his mouth and abused him with very opprobious language'. A month later the persistent Firmin took Butcher's 'Hatt from off his Head and threw it on the ground several times'. Finally, displaying ingenious cunning, Firmin invited the by now well-battered Butcher to go to The Horn Inn with him, where he would buy him a half-pint of wine. Naturally suspicious, Butcher asked if he was in earnest. Firmin replied 'yes', but then burst out 'Damn you I'll do my message here' and, attempting to take hold of Butcher's nose but 'missing his design', punched him on the nose.

Another picture of crime in 18th century Braintree is painted by a story which has more than a touch of Oliver Twist about it. The tale is best told in the words of 15 year old Sarah Purchas, who stated that 'about 2 am she was under the Horsing Block before the shop of Edward Tabor in Braintree, where she hid herself upon seeing of a man coming along; that her Master, Joseph Craknel, after she was in bed, had made her rise, and ordered her to go to Edward Tabor's house, to get in through the window, and open the door for him. That when she had been there, she could not open the window. She went back and told him she could not open it; that he returned with her to the house, broke some glass in the window, and put her in through it; that she then opened the back door, where her Master stood, who bid her go home to bed, and said he would do what he had a mind to do, and that there was another coming to pain, that he at the same time gave her 3½d that she might hold her tongue, and that the next morning gave her about ½lb of sugar, bidding her to say nothing of what she had done'.

As well as house-breaking, there were rich pickings to be made on the roads. The road from Braintree to Witham was notorious for highwaymen during the 17th century. Often less spectacular methods were used, such as in 1817 when a package containing £10 in notes was taken from the Braintree coach as it stood outside The Horn Inn. Punishment for serious offences was harsh, and local criminals were sent either to the County Gaol at Chelmsford or to the convict hulks moored at Woolwich, Portsmouth, and Chatham. The Braintree 'Lock-Up' or Cage housed only minor offenders, mostly riotous drunks. The Parish Cage was originally next to the old workhouse in Market Street. When this was pulled down, in 1838, the Board of Guardians paid for a new Cage in New Street. It still stands today—a reminder of rougher days.

At a Meeting of the Select Vestry of the Parish of BRAINTREE, it was unanimously agreed that the following RULES be adopted for the future relief of all Vagrants passing through the said Parish.

1. The Vestry Clerk shall keep a Register, ruled with columns, in which shall be entered the name, age, and general description of each Vagrant, applying for relief.

2. No money shall be given to a Vagrant, except in especial cases, at the discretion of the Overseer.

3. No Vagrant shall be admitted into the Vagrant House without a ticket, signed by one of the parish officers, in this form—

Braintree, 18
Admit the Bearer into the Vagrant House.
Overseer.

specifying the hour at which it is granted, and if the ticket be not delivered within one hour it shall become void.

4. All persons, upwards of 12 years of age, to receive, subject to the discretion of the Overseer, not exceeding—

Six ounces of Bread and Half-pint of Beer.

Under Twelve Years of Age.

Four ounces of Bread and Half-pint of Beer.

5. Any person remaining after suitable refreshment, unless from illness, shall be set to hard work.

6. All persons shall be discharged every morning, in summer at Six o'clock, and in winter at Eight o'clock, unless prevented by illness.

7. Any Vagrant found begging in Braintree, after being discharged, shall be apprehended.

8. No smoking allowed.

9. All Vagrants shall be searched on their admittance, and if money or other property be found in their possession, notice shall be given to the parish officers.

10. Men and women shall be kept in separate wards; but male children under the age of six years shall be allowed to sleep with their mothers.

Braintree, April 21, 1828.

JOSCELYNE, PRINTER, BRAINTREE AND COGGESHALL.

LEFT: Select Vestry rules for the relief of vagrants, 1828. (ERO/JA) RIGHT: The New Street Lock-up or Cage, built 1838. BELOW: The former County Courthouse, now the Library.

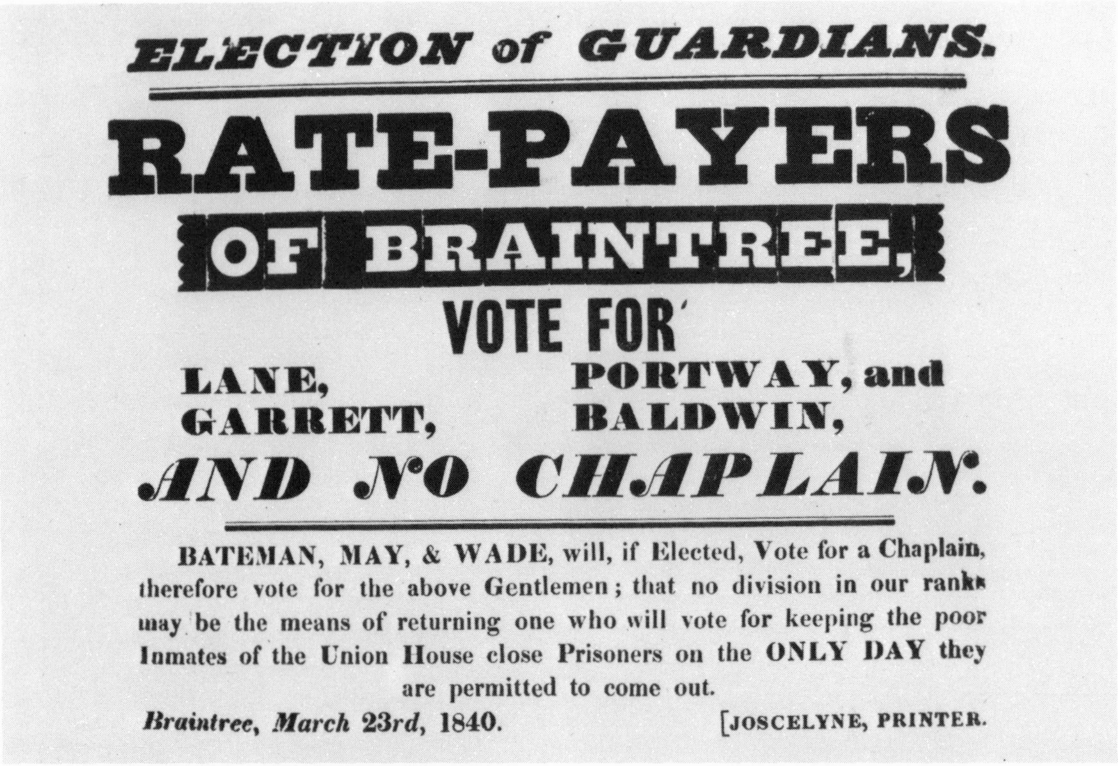

ELECTION of GUARDIANS.

RATE-PAYERS

OF BRAINTREE,

VOTE FOR

LANE, GARRETT, PORTWAY, and BALDWIN,

AND NO CHAPLAIN.

BATEMAN, MAY, & WADE, will, if Elected, Vote for a Chaplain, therefore vote for the above Gentlemen; that no division in our ranks may be the means of returning one who will vote for keeping the poor Inmates of the Union House close Prisoners on the ONLY DAY they are permitted to come out.

Braintree, March 23rd, 1840. [JOSCELYNE, PRINTER.

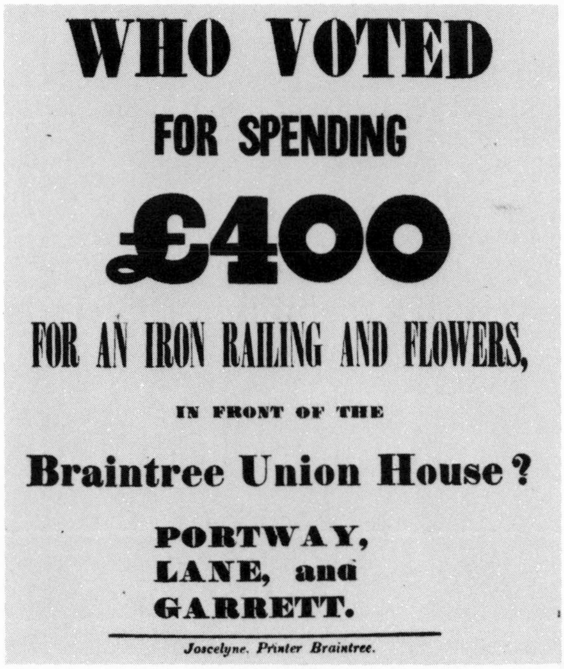

WHO VOTED

FOR SPENDING

£400

FOR AN IRON RAILING AND FLOWERS,

IN FRONT OF THE

Braintree Union House?

PORTWAY, LANE, and GARRETT.

Joscelyne, Printer Braintree.

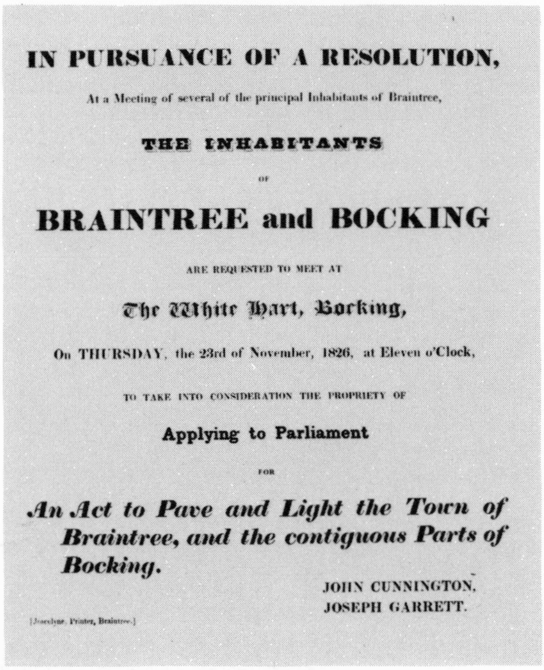

IN PURSUANCE OF A RESOLUTION,

At a Meeting of several of the principal Inhabitants of Braintree,

THE INHABITANTS

OF

BRAINTREE and BOCKING

ARE REQUESTED TO MEET AT

The White Hart, Bocking,

On THURSDAY, the 23rd of November, 1826, at Eleven o'Clock,

TO TAKE INTO CONSIDERATION THE PROPRIETY OF

Applying to Parliament

FOR

An Act to Pave and Light the Town of Braintree, and the contiguous Parts of Bocking.

JOHN CUNNINGTON,
JOSEPH GARRETT.

[Joscelyne, Printer, Braintree.]

ABOVE: Election poster, Board of Guardians, 1840. (ERO/JA) LEFT: Poster criticising spending on the Union Workhouse (now St Michael's Hospital), 1845. (ERO/JA) RIGHT: Poster for public meeting to consider paving and lighting the town, 1826. (ERO/JA)

ABOVE: Fire engine ordered by Braintree Lighting and Watching Inspectors, 1845. (ERO/JA) BELOW: Braintree Fire Brigade, c1890. (NG)

BRAINTREE, ESSEX.

PARTICULARS AND CONDITIONS OF SALE

OF THAT

WIDELY KNOWN ESTABLISHMENT,

THE

"WHITE HART" HOTEL,

BOCKING,

WITH GARDENS,

AND

SEVERAL PLOTS OF

FREEHOLD BUILDING LAND,

For Sale by Auction, with Immediate Possession,

ON THE PREMISES,

ON WEDNESDAY, THE 21ST OF APRIL, 1869,

At Three o'Clock.

SOLICITORS—Messrs. DUFFIELD & BRUTY,
6, Tokenhouse Yard, E.C., and Chelmsford.

AUCTIONEERS—Mr. BENJAMIN T. THURGOOD,
Saffron Walden.
Mr. G. H. DURRANT,
36, Poultry, E.C.

PARTICULARS.

The several lots are delineated on Plan annexed.

LOT 1.

THE "WHITE HART" HOTEL, BOCKING,

Commandingly situate in the centre of the Manufacturing Towns of

BRAINTREE AND BOCKING,

At the Junction of four of the principal turnpike roads, within five minutes' walk of the Great Eastern Railway Station, whence London by two routes and all the principal towns in the Eastern and Midland counties are easily accessible. One of the largest corn and cattle markets is held on the Wednesday in each week, and extensive manufactory of silk and crape are carried on in both parishes.

The Premises, unusually compact and in thorough repair, are of a most substantial character and conveniently arranged for carrying on an extensive trade; the internal accomodation may be briefly described as follows:—

FIVE PRIVATE SITTING ROOMS,

An excellent **COMMERCIAL ROOM,** with two windows, one having bay 24ft by 14ft., a **READING ROOM,** to which a Subscription Room is attached, a **COFFEE ROOM,**

COMMODIOUS BAR,

Handsomely appointed with plate glass front, mahogany fittings, Parlor, Lavatory, Kitchen, with every convenience, communicating with well fitted Store Room, Scullery, Butler's Pantry, Larder, and Dairy.

The First Floor is approached by three different Staircases, one of which is entirely private, and there are in all

FIFTEEN WELL-ARRANGED BED AND DRESSING ROOMS,

Two W.C.'s, and Spacious Landing.

Attached is a HANDSOME STRUCTURE of comparative recent erection, comprising Five Lofty and Spacious Rooms, thus appropriated—

A NOBLE BALL, CONCERT, OR LECTURE ROOM,

52 by 22 feet, with spacious Windows, Fireplaces at either end, with marble mantels, enriched cornice, and ventilator in roof. A ROOM UNDER, 36 feet by 22 feet, in which the Magistrates for the division hold their Sitting, which is calculated to make the

MOST HANDSOME BILLIARD ROOM IN THE COUNTY.

To these Rooms are attached others, each 16 feet by 12 feet, of similar character and decorations, now used as Bed and Dining Rooms, but convertible to Refreshment or Retiring Rooms at pleasure.

This Building communicates with the Hotel, but has in addition an independent Entrance Hall, with handsome Staircase, also Billiard or Saddle Room.

The access to the Vaulted Cellars is easy; there is a Cask Entrance, and they afford ample space for carrying on the

WHOLESALE WINE AND SPIRIT TRADE

In connection with the Hotel, which is much needed in the town and neighbourhood.

THE YARDS are approached from the Street through an arched Gateway enclosed with Folding Gates, having spacious Stabling, Loose Boxes for Hunters, Lock-up and Open Coach-houses, Lofts, Granary, and every convenience.

THE TAP, recently put in thorough repair, with

CAPITAL CELLARAGE AND BREWHOUSE ATTACHED,

Immediately adjoins the Hotel, but has the advantage of a separate entrance from the Coggeshall Road, and the present lucrative trade might be greatly enhanced by converting it into a Gin Palace, for which its accommodation and position admirably fit it.

It is at present in the occupation of Mr. Richard Peters, who pays the moderate sum of £20 per annum, and is under the customary notice to quit on the 24th day of June next, should a purchaser desire it.

Gas and water are laid on throughout the Premises, and there is also an excellent pump.

The Tenant's fixtures specified in the inventory which will be produced at the time of sale, shall be taken by valuation in the usual way. The furniture, stock, old wines, horses, carriages, and utensils in trade can be taken or rejected at the purchaser's option.

Sale particulars of the White Hart, Bocking, 1869.

Pulpit and Soapbox

The parish church, dedicated to St Michael, was built soon after the birth of the 'new town' at the crossroads. Today's church bears little resemblance to that first building, but the tower and east chancel do include Roman bricks—a clue to the possible presence of a Roman settlement on the site—and are believed to date from the 12th century.

As Braintree grew, so the church was, bit by bit, enlarged. The necessary funds were often provided by the many pilgrims who passed through the town on their way into Suffolk and Norfolk and by the town's clothiers who were growing rich. But when restoration was needed in the mid-16th century another method of fund-raising was found as the church was turned into a theatre.

Three mystery plays were performed: *St Swithin,* in the 'great summer festival' in 1532; *St Andrew,* in 1534; and *Placy Dacy, alias Evestacy,* also in 1534. Like pageants in the great mediaeval Mystery Cycles at York and Chester, the plays were performed and produced by the members of the trade guilds in the town. Each group had an appropriate task, with the carpenters building the stage and the drapers making the costumes, though props were generally sparse and representational rather than realistic.

Sometimes performers and supplies were hired, as these entries in the Chelmsford Churchwardens' Accounts show:

'To the mynstralls for going to Branktree.................... 16s 0d
For the plaiers dinner at Branktree at the show there.......... 7s 8d
For drinks brought to the Friars........................... 8d'

This seems to support the allegations of an early historian who believed that the Braintree plays 'tended not only to gratify the eye and the ear, but great preparations were likewise made for satisfying the belly'.

The connection between the church and drama does not end here. Nicholas Udall, who was vicar of Braintree from 1537 to 1544, açhieved fame by writing what is generally accepted to be the first English Comedy, *Ralph Roister Doister.* He was at the same time headmaster of Eton—until dismissed for misconduct—and it is doubtful whether he found much time to visit his parish. Nevertheless, it upheld the town's dramatic tradition.

But for many this period of religious history was marked by tragedy. During the

Catholic revival under Queen Mary, or 'Bloody Mary', several local people were executed for following the Protestant faith. In 1555, William Pygot, a youth of 19, was publicly burnt to death in the Hyde Field in the town centre. The following year, another five men and one woman, all of Bocking, suffered the same agonising fate.

About this time a group of worshippers made a break from the established church, starting a tradition of Nonconformity which has marked the town's history. It seems to have started around 1550 when an independent congregation, drawing heavily on Braintree for support, became one of the first in the country to separate from the Church of England.

Queen Elizabeth came to the throne in 1558 and, faced with problems of religious strife, passed a law enforcing church attendance. Her reign saw the rise of Puritanism, a movement which objected to the Church of England not being based solely on the Bible. The movement was closely linked with the cloth trade and in both Braintree and Bocking large numbers were prosecuted for non-attendance at church. Some were charged with being 'in houses during Service', implying that they were holding secret and illegal dissenting meetings.

This strong Puritan connection was recorded by John Ray in his book on English proverbs:

'Braintree for the Pure,
Bocking for the Poor,
Coggeshall for the Jeering Town,
Kelvedon for the Whore'.

With prosecutions running high in the town in the 1620s and 1630s, a famous Puritan preacher, Thomas Hooker, began visiting Braintree. He was later to form the 'Braintree Company' which sailed to New England in the *Lyon* in 1632. Embarking just 12 years after the *Mayflower*, the *Lyon* carried a heavy contingent of Essex people who made their mark on the New World.

The Braintree Company—so called because the voyage was organised in the town and included several local people—first set foot on North American soil at Mount Wollaston, a tiny settlement close to the site of present-day Boston. Many of the company later moved on to Newetowne, but it seems likely that some stayed, or returned, for in 1640 Wollaston was renamed Braintree.

Several former Braintree (Essex) families have played an important part in the history of the United States. Henry Adams, who became the first town clerk of Braintree, Massachusetts, was the great-grandfather of John Adams, the second President of the United States. He, in turn, was father of John Quincy Adams, the sixth President. John Bridge, one of those who moved on to Newetowne, started a school there, which was the forerunner of Harvard University.

By the end of the century, there was a growing spirit of toleration. In 1689, the Toleration Act permitted dissenting congregations to gather, provided they registered their place of worship. By 1703 there were at least four of these licensed Houses of Prayer in the town at the homes of Thomas Livermore, Robert Austen, John Earle, and John Livermore. At Bocking End regular meetings had been held for many years in a large barn belonging to John English. It has even been suggested that John Bunyan, author of *Pilgrim's Progress,* preached there during his visits to the English family.

In 1707, the Bocking Nonconformists built their own Meeting House. The original red-brick building, with gabled roof and leaded lights, seated about 800 and survived until 1818. Its replacement, at Bocking End, still stands today. At the start of the 19th century there were 553 Bocking dissenters and an equally large group in Braintree, who attended either the Bocking End Chapel or the Anabaptists' Meeting House in the town.

By mid-century, a staggering three-quarters of those attending church service in Braintree were Nonconformists. St Michael's was only half full, but the chapels were bursting at the seams. The Rev Thomas Craig at Bocking End Independent Chapel was pulling in a congregation of well over 1,000 each Sunday. This was more than double the combined total of the congregations at Braintree and Bocking parish churches.

Not far behind in popularity was the Independent Chapel in London Road where the Rev John Carter regularly preached to as many as 1,000. Only half that many attended the Baptist Chapel in Coggeshall Road. The smallest gathering was at the Friends' Meeting House in Rayne Road. Here the congregation numbered fewer than 30, even though the Quakers had been established in the town since the 17th century.

By contrast, the national picture showed that Nonconformists were slightly outnumbered by those attending the Church of England. It is hardly surprising then, that the opposition of Braintree and Bocking dissenters to the payment of the rate levied by the established church became a test case. Starting as a local issue in Bocking in 1834, this dispute broadened into a national argument which was dubbed the 'Braintree Church Rates Case'. It was not resolved until a House of Lords ruling established a major victory for the principle of religious freedom.

It began when an attempt was made to raise money for the repair of Bocking church. Samuel Courtauld, supported by other dissenters, circulated a leaflet opposing the levy. This led to a majority vote in the vestry against the rate. But this was only a temporary solution. Two years later the churchwardens insisted on collecting the rate even though the Nonconformists had again achieved a majority in the vestry.

The next stage was the courts and Veley v Burder: the former, a churchwarden suing for the rate; the latter, a dissenter who refused to pay. The case dragged through three courts, with the final verdict favouring the dissenters but leaving an important loophole through which, in 1841, the churchwardens tried to wriggle. So, once more to the courts until, finally, in 1853, a House of Lords ruling confirmed that a rate could only be levied by a majority vote in the vestry.

Samuel Courtauld's role in this struggle for religious freedom was recognised both locally and nationally. In 1881, his obituary in *The Times* read: 'Had the death of Mr Courtauld happened some 30 or 40 years ago a popular hero would have passed away...the Braintree case practically gave the law of church rates in every shape its "coup de grace" '.

Courtauld was also a fighter for political freedom. The family's historian believes that it is 'certain' that Samuel was in the forefront of local Liberal-Radical politics during the 1830s. This period saw the first extension of the franchise beyond a tiny elite. To understand what it meant to Braintree we need to look at the political situation a century earlier.

For the people of Braintree national politics were a distant matter. The entire county was represented by just two members at Westminster. Yet the boroughs—Harwich, Colchester, and Maldon—each returned two MPs. Yet for most this made little practical difference since they had no vote at all, the franchise being restricted to freeholders with more than 40s a year. There were few enough of them in the town.

Eighteenth century elections were notoriously corrupt, with candidates spending vast amounts to woo voters. There was no secret ballot, and landowners studied the poll books to make sure their tenants had voted for the 'right' man. In the early part of the century the county members were generally Whigs, but in 1734 two Tories were returned. Thirty years later a compromise was reached by which one member was returned by each party. This undemocratic arrangement lasted until 1810.

There had been earlier moves for political reform. In 1740, 30 men from Braintree and Halstead published a 'Reform Resolution', but they were too respectful—and frightened—to carry it through. It was not easy when their livelihood depended on those in power. When national reform finally arrived with the 1832 Act, the franchise was scarcely extended. This act carefully preserved the principle that Parliament represented property, not people. In Braintree a few householders may have gained the vote, but there were still just 107 votes in a town of some 3,500 people.

Disenchantment with the Reform Act led some to political agitation. Samuel Courtauld played a part in the town's lively Reform Association. This spoke largely for the well-to-do who still had no vote. The bulk of the population could do little. Although there was some interest in Chartism among the Courtauld weavers, the leadership was firmly in the hands of the respectable artisans and tradesmen, and there are no records of violence.

One thing the Act did do for Braintree was to make it the principal polling station for the North Essex Division, with slightly more votes cast there than at Colchester. This was considered a great boost to the town's prestige, even though so few of the townspeople could vote. John Cunnington believed it had 'added more to the town's importance than anything else of late', and it was this which urged him to write a short history of the town in 1833.

The first election after the Act was in December 1832 in the Hyde Field—the site of today's Town Hall—and it attracted a great crowd. An eye-witness described the scene: 'The election only lasted three days. There was a tent put up with a platform at the front, which was called the "hustings". The voters were for the most part farmers, and arrived on horseback. They formed themselves into two processions, each headed by a band of music, carrying flags, one blue coats and the other yellow. They made no secret of whom they were going to vote for. The candidates made speeches in the field. Afterwards they gave a dinner for each man who voted for them'. The Tories carried the day by a small margin thanks largely to their support in the countryside, though Braintree itself was mostly Whig.

With Parliamentary politics closed to them, the working classes found other ways of helping themselves. Early in the century labour organisation was prohibited by the Combination Laws. But meetings were held under the euphemistic title of Friendly Societies, such as the Shoemakers' Society which met at the White Hart. Yet, even after the Combination Laws were repealed there was little sign of trade union activity in the town.

Among the Braintree weavers—at least as far as Courtaulds is concerned—union activity did not have an impact until the end of the century. An attempted strike by power-loom weavers at Halstead in 1860 provided a warning to other Courtauld workers at Braintree and Bocking. It was firmly put down by an angry Samuel Courtauld who dismissed the men involved.

When another group of workers, the agricultural labourers, tried to set up a union in north Essex in 1836 they too were soon defeated. The union was formed in the Spring with the aim of fixing a minimum wage of 2s a day. Although membership soon topped 1,200, by July the combined forces of the church, the farmers, and the *Essex Standard* newspaper had destroyed what the latter described as a 'wrong and unchristian alliance'. Frustrated, a few farmworkers turned to fire-raising. In a six week spell in the spring of 1844, eight fires were started in and around Braintree. There was simply no other way of protesting against low wages, high unemployment, and the harsh poor laws.

Rural union activity was not revived until the 1870s when—under the leadership of a radical farmer from Wethersfield, Charles Jay—north Essex farmworkers joined the recently formed National Agricultural Labourers Union. A farmers' lock-out soon broke the North Essex Branch, but not before the union had arranged the migration of several thousand men to northern England and had been given a taste of trade unionism which was to prove useful in later years.

One form of working class organisation which did make enormous strides at this time was the Cooperative movement. This had started in Rochdale in 1844 when 28 men opened a Cooperative store. Twenty years after the 'Rochdale Pioneers', a group of Braintree weavers raised the idea of a similar distributive society. Preliminary talks took place in the house of a Mr Cowell in South Street and afterwards in The George Inn. A 1s subscription raised enough capital to open a shop in a weaver's cottage at Pound End. The first stock of supplies—tea, sugar, butter, soap, and a few other household items—soon sold out.

As the Society expanded the shop was moved to Swan Street in the centre of town. In the 1870s they began to bake and sell bread and distribute coal through a Coal Club. A further move followed, this time to Bocking End, where there was a Savings

Bank and a Workman's Club. This building was extended in 1905 and was occupied by the Coop Bank until quite recently, when the building—complete with distinctive clock tower—was demolished to make way for a supermarket.

ABOVE: St Michael's, c1900. (ERO/JA) BELOW: William Pygot, Protestant, burnt to death, c1555, from Town Hall Murals. (ERO/JA)

ABOVE: Sailing of the Braintree Company in the Lyon, 1632, from Town Hall Murals. (ERO/JA) BELOW: The Meeting House, Bocking End, c1848. (ERO/JA) INSET: John Bunyan, friend of the English family of Bocking. (ERO/JA)

LEFT: Bocking End Congregational Chapel, 1981. RIGHT: Braintree New Chapel, 1833. (ERO/J) CENTRE: Bocking End Congregational Chapel and School, c1900. (ERO/JA) BELOW: London Road Chapel, c1900. (ERO/JA) INSET: Rev John Carter. (ERO/JA)

ABOVE: Free Church and Coggeshall Road, c1900. (ERO/JA) LEFT: Sketch of Methodist Church, Rayne Road. (DW) RIGHT: Monument to Bishop Gauden of Bocking. (ERO/JA) CENTRE: St Mary's, Bocking. (NG) BELOW: St Peter's, Bocking.

BRAINTREE! BRAINTREE!

Great Liberal Demonstration

MASS MEETING

IN THE

CORN EXCHANGE, BRAINTREE

ON FRIDAY, MARCH 11th, 1904.

The Chair will be taken at 7.30 p.m. by

J. H. TRITTON, ESQ., J.P.

WHO WILL BE SUPPORTED BY

AUGUSTINE BIRRELL, ESQ., K.C.,

President National Liberal Federation,

J. A. PEASE, ESQ., M.P.

E. B. BARNARD, Esq. W. C. BONNERJEE, Esq.
T. R. BETHELL, Esq. JOS SMITH, Jun., Esq., J.P.
G. C. MABERLEY, Esq. FREDK. WEST, Esq., C.C.

Programme.

1. **Chairman's Address.**
2. **Mr. Birrell's Speech.**
3. **First Resolution.**—

That this meeting emphatically declares that the present Government neither possesses nor deserves the confidence of the Country. It has wantonly threatened changes in our Fiscal Policy involving Protection, which would increase the price of food and would be deeply injurious to the National strength, contentment and well being of the people. It has also enormously increased taxation without insuring the National Safety, and it has passed an Education Act which conflicts with Religious Freedom and Liberal Principles.

Further that this meeting strongly condemns the Government sanction to a form of Slavery by the importation of indentured Chinese labourers into the Transvaal which, besides reversing our National Traditions on that important question, will also tend to exclude British working men from the South African Colonies.

To be moved by J. A. Pease, Esq., M.P.
To be seconded by W. C. Bonnerjee, Esq.
To be supported by E. B. Barnard, Esq.

4. **Second Resolution.**—

That the best thanks of this meeting be given to Augustine Birrell, Esq., for his presence and speech and also to J. H. Tritton, Esq., for presiding over the meeting.

To be moved by T. R. Bethell, Esq.
To be seconded by Fredk. West, Esq.
To be supported by Joseph Smith, Jun., Esq., who will also put it to the Meeting.

ABOVE: Braintree Co-operative Society Central Stores: annual outing. (ERO/JA) LEFT: Liberal Party poster, 1904. (ERO/JA) RIGHT: Co-operative Society's new Central Stores, Bocking End. (ERO/JA)

The King's Highway

In the course of his nine-day morris dance from London to Norwich in 1599, William Kempe, who played the Fool in Shakespeare's plays, found himself on the road from Chelmsford to Braintree. 'Road' is hardly the right word though. For Kempe, who was far from being a timid man, described this highway as 'flanked with thick woods and so full of deep holes that he was thankful to reach Braintree at all'.

He had good reason to be thankful. Not only did he risk breaking his neck by falling into a pot-hole, but he was also in danger of being attacked and robbed. Highwaymen were known to ply their trade on the roads around Braintree. There was Daniel Baisie, for example, who confessed, in May 1603, that 'he with two others stood in the King's highway by Faulkbourne Park, that leadeth from Witham to Braintree, and there intended to rob such of His Majesty's subjects as should pass that way'. This was at a time when the journey from Braintree to London was at its most hazardous, passing as it did through the dense and dark Epping Forest, one of the most notorious haunts of the highway robber.

The Elizabethans did little to improve their roads. They remained in much the same state as they had been for centuries — overgrown and pock-marked with holes, 'sloughs', and 'noisome corners'. The smaller roads were no more than deeply-rutted tracks, almost impassable in winter. Upkeep fell to the parishes, who often preferred to forget their duty. Landowners and householders were supposed to either work on the roads themselves or to find substitutes. The regularity with which cases of neglecting to do one's work on the roads appeared before the magistrates does much to explain why the roads were in such a bad way.

During the 17th century the Select Vestry maintained the roads and bridges in the town. But as their power and efficiency waned towards the end of the century, the roads deteriorated once more. Another cause of neglect was the number of disputes between Braintree and Bocking over which parish was responsible for which bit of road. One dispute became so entangled that it took the intervention of the Quarter Sessions Court before the following agreement was made in April 1678: 'Whereas there hath lately been some difference between the inhabitants of Braintree and Bocking concerning the repairs of the highwayes leading from Coggeshall towards Rayne... It is agreed that Bocking repairs both sides of the highway from White Hart Corner towards Rayne and Braintree repairs from White Hart Corner towards Coggeshall.'

Braintree and Bocking were still remote places by the end of the 17th century. The main road across Essex led from Harwich to London. Yet Ogilby's map of this road in 1670 shows only a by-road to Braintree branching off a mile north of Witham. Not until the granting of turnpike powers—which allowed a toll to be collected from road users and spent on road repairs—was there any marked improvement in the state of roads. In 1695 an Act of Parliament was obtained to enclose and repair the London-Harwich road. Later Acts extended the turnpikes to the roads around Braintree. The growth of the market, and the need to transport goods, stimulated major improvements in the 18th century, and the Essex Turnpike Trust took over the management of roads from Braintree to Colchester, Chelmsford, the Hedinghams, Halstead, and Witham via the Notleys. There were toll gates at Braintree (Coggeshall Road), Leighs, White Notley, Chipping Hill, Gosfield, and the Hedinghams.

Elizabethan travellers went mostly by horse or on foot. So it was not until horse-drawn vehicles became widespread that there was any urgent need to improve the roads. Carts were the first to be used, while passenger coaches were not common until the middle of the 18th century. Carriers were taking loads of cloth from Braintree to London as early as the 1600s, though most was taken to Maldon and from there taken by sea. At that time it was said that 'the carriers of Braintree and Bocking do lodge at the sign of the Tabard in Gracious Street, near the Conduit. They do come on Thursdays and go away on Fridays'. The journey took several days since the broad-wheeled wagons went at no more than walking pace.

By the middle of the 18th century, three wagons a week left Braintree for London, and by 1775 this had risen to four. One enterprising Bocking carrier started a 'Flying Stage Wagon' which raced to Leadenhall Street in just 14 hours. The carrying trade grew after the Napoleonic Wars, and by 1837 there were 19 wagons leaving London for Braintree on every day of the week except Sunday and Monday. They left in the afternoon to allow London merchants to make morning deliveries and so the drivers could get out of London before putting up for the night. Each driver had his favourite 'baiting house' (to 'bait' means to stop at an inn, originally to feed the horses). Often there would be 20 or 30 teams of horses at one inn. But the railway, which reached Braintree in the 1840s, was to change all this. For a while the carriers complemented the railway by concentrating on the cross-country routes, but, steadily and inevitably, as the rail network spread they were forced out of business.

The first Essex route to be served by public transport was the London to Harwich road, where a coach service began in 1711. But this road only came within seven miles of Braintree. By 1744 things were rather better, with coaches leaving London for Braintree on Tuesdays, Thursdays, and Saturdays in the winter, and Mondays, Wednesdays, and Fridays in the summer. The journey involved about seven hours of being jolted up and down on hard seats and, for those travelling 'outside', no protection from the weather. Nevertheless it was a passenger service, and in 1772 Muilman, describing the town as a 'great thoroughfare from London into Suffolk and Norfolk', said the Bury, Norwich, and Sudbury coaches passed through it each day.

In 1794 the fare for the seven hour torture to London was 12s single inside, and 8s outside. Although highwaymen had almost disappeared by the middle of the century, coach travel was still hazardous. The passengers inside were tightly packed, while those outside had to hang on for their lives. According to the price you paid, you chose between being left behind at a sharp corner or suffering mild concussion from the repeated meeting of head and coach roof. Wherever you sat, there was one part of the anatomy which did not escape—for iron tyres and poor springing ensured that no passenger would want to sit down again for several hours afterwards. To make matters worse, there were frequent cases of racing or furious driving by coachmen—who also often took extra passengers surreptitiously—and, consequently, of runaway coaches. The Bury coach is once said to have gone through Braintree at a great pace with the only outside passenger, an elderly woman, shouting 'murder' all the way. Overloading was a common cause of accidents. On 25 March 1775 the Norwich coach, with six passengers on top, overturned in Bocking Church Street. Two passengers each broke a leg and several were reported to be 'much hurt'.

By the 1820s, Braintree's days of isolation were over. As well as the many coaches from London into East Anglia, there were three local coaches starting from the town each day. There was also a stage coach which left for Halstead at eight o'clock in the evening and which returned at 6.30 am. The journey to London had been reduced to five hours, making it possible for manufacturers, bankers, and businessmen to leave early for London, do their business there, and return the same day. The faster coaches also put Braintree into closer contact with the rest of the country by establishing a faster postal service.

The popularity of coach travel was a great boost to the inns which served as picking-up points. The Horn was the chief coaching inn at Braintree, while in Bocking it was the White Hart or The Woolpack. The Horn, with its central carriageway and large stables, was the ideal station for the London coaches on their way into Suffolk and Norfolk. The number of men and boys who gave their occupation as ostlers or stable-lads shows how the coaches brought employment to the town. Shopkeepers benefitted too, especially the high-class grocers and drapers who needed to order fancy goods from London. One such tradesman was Augustus Portway—whose billheads described him as 'linen draper, grocer, liquor merchant, family mourning, and funeral furnisher'—who kept shop in Great Square. His customers included the local gentry and nobility, and he relied heavily on the stage coaches to bring luxury goods from London, as for example, when Louis XVIII of France visited Gosfield Hall and the hostess wanted some very special foodstuffs to set before him. Thanks to the coaches Augustus Portway was able to meet the order.

The 'golden age' of coaching was in the 1830s and early 1840s when the coaches were spurred on to faster times and fuller services by the threat of the railway. By 1836 the time to London had been reduced to four hours and forty minutes, with an average speed of just over 10 mph. By this time there were no less than 31 licensed coaches and two mail coaches running from Chelmsford to London. These connected with four from Chelmsford to Braintree and Sudbury, and a further coach to Sudbury through Bocking. But horse-power could not match steam, and the end had to come. The last Colchester-London coach ran in 1843. The *Bury Times* from the Half Moon in Bury to the Green Dragon in Bishopsgate ceased in March 1848—just a few months before the iron track of the railway reached Braintree.

ABOVE: John Wood's Sudbury, Hedingham & Braintree Coach painted by J. Cordrey, c1820. (ERO/JA) BELOW: London Road, c1900. (NG)

ABOVE: Braintree's chief coaching inn, The Horn, photographed c1900.
(ERO/JA) BELOW: Joscelyne's horse-drawn removal van. (CR)

FLETCHER LD.

OPPOSITE ABOVE: Motor-cars and horse-drawn carts share a peaceful Bank Street. (NG) CENTRE: London Road c1920, before William Julien Courtauld Hospital was built. (NG) BELOW: A traffic hazard in Church Street, Bocking, (ERO/JA) ABOVE: Hoppit Bridge, Notley Road, (ERO/JA) BELOW: Jubilee Oak, Coggeshall Road c1910. (ERO/JA)

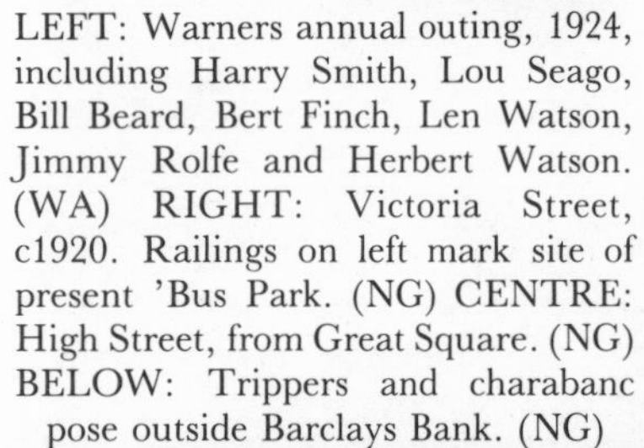

LEFT: Warners annual outing, 1924, including Harry Smith, Lou Seago, Bill Beard, Bert Finch, Len Watson, Jimmy Rolfe and Herbert Watson. (WA) RIGHT: Victoria Street, c1920. Railings on left mark site of present 'Bus Park. (NG) CENTRE: High Street, from Great Square. (NG) BELOW: Trippers and charabanc pose outside Barclays Bank. (NG)

The Railway Arrives

Long before 8am on Monday 7 October 1848, a crowd of excited people began to gather at Braintree Station. Many had rushed there, leaving half-eaten breakfasts. There was a buzz of expectancy as the hands on the new station clock reached eight o'clock. For at that time, precisely, the first passenger train to travel the Maldon, Witham and Braintree Railway pulled out of Maldon Station. Just 40 minutes later, hundreds of heads turned to see the smoking engine come round the corner and cheered as the first railway passengers alighted at Braintree.

This historic day had taken a long time to arrive. The first scheme for a railway to Braintree had been suggested in February 1824. On that date a 'very respectable and numerous body of capitalists' had met in Witham with a view to setting up a railway company. They got as far as finding an engineer to survey the 14 miles of country and made an estimate of the cost. But their enthusiasm was dealt a blow when the engineer failed to attend a later meeting and, soon after, the matter was dropped.

A year later another group of hopeful men put forward the idea of a line running from Colchester to Braintree and Halstead. They were tradesmen who hoped that a railway would provide cheap transport for goods to market, and for coal which was brought to Braintree from Maldon by cart. This scheme too never got beyond a pipe-dream. However it showed the enthusiasm of local businessmen for a railway even before the first piece of track was laid in Essex. The first line in the county—running from Mile End to Romford—was not opened until 1839. As the years went by, it stretched eastwards reaching Colchester in 1843. This brought the railway to within seven miles of Braintree, the nearest point being Witham.

This was enough to inject new enthusiasm into the inhabitants of the town for a rail link. The first step was taken in February 1845, when the Maldon, Witham, and Braintree Railway Company was registered. A private bill was passed through Parliament and by June 1846 the MWBR Company, with a capital of £200,000, was ready to start building. The proposed line was to be 12 miles long, running along the Blackwater valley from Maldon to Witham, where a level-crossing was planned over the Eastern Counties Railway, and on to Braintree following the river Brain.

The company's first task was to find an engineer. They chose Joseph Locke, a capable man who had worked with the Stephensons on the early Liverpool-Manchester railway. They also engaged a surveyor and suggested the deepening of the river at

Maldon, as it was thought necessary to build a dock beside the station there. However the independence of the MWBR Company did not last long. In 1847 it was absorbed into the Eastern Counties Railway, who bought out the shareholders. The takeover was complete when George Hudson, the notorious and crooked 'Railway King', became director of the MWBR Company.

In March of that year the contract was given to Thomas Jackson, who described himself as a 'practical mechanic', who employed 3,500 men. By May more than 500 labourers—the famous railway 'navvies'—were laying the line from Witham to Notley. Two months later the workforce had risen to over 1,000, or the equivalent of a quarter of the population of Braintree. Since there was little in the way of earth-moving equipment, and the early locomotives could manage only the gentlest of gradients, railway-building depended on these huge bands of men wielding pick and shovel. By the beginning of summer, cuttings and embankments had been dug and some of the permanent way laid. Bridge-building was in progress and the whole project was going smoothly. But then the summer rains began and work was halted, and the unemployed navvies spent their time walking aimlessly around Witham.

An invasion by a large group of rough men must have been a worrying time for the local population. The residents of some of the small towns and villages along the railway were often outnumbered by the navvies. One has only to think of the effect of 1,000 men setting up camp at Cressing or the Notleys to imagine the problems and disturbance that railway-building brought. Especially as these were unruly and physically powerful men, who had little else to do with their money but spend it on drink. When they did eventually move on, it was probably only the shopkeepers and publicans who were sorry to see the back of them.

In the autumn of 1847, with the rains now over, work was started with new vigour, in the hope of opening in the spring. The cast-iron girders for the bridges at Witham and Maldon—according to one report 'the largest, with one exception, that have ever been cast'—were placed in position. A 'handsome station' with a new approach road was built at Braintree. Yet, despite this, heavy rain prevented the line from opening in the middle of August 1848. A few days later, though, a goods train ran from Maldon to Braintree, and in one September week the line carried 300 tons of coal and over 350 tons of freight.

The Company and the people of Braintree now anxiously awaited the report from the Board of Trade Inspector, which would give the go-ahead for passenger traffic. The report was published on 30 September 1848. The Inspector wrote: 'the earth works on the line are not heavy and the slopes stand well... two bridges which are public roads are carried by girders of sufficient strength. Six viaducts carry the railway over rivers and brooks, they are of timber of the simplest construction, the permanent way is laid double throughout. There are four stations, Bulford (which was renamed Cressing in 1911), Braintree, Wickham Mill, and Maldon. I found the line in good order and free from all obstructions and I consider it may be opened for the conveyance of passengers'.

For the ordinary working people of Braintree, the first historic journey was a spectator event only. But a few days later, an excursion train ran to and from Braintree Fair at a reduced price, giving many local people their first ever taste of train travel. At first, there were five trains a day from Braintree. The single fare to Maldon was 2s 6d first class, 2s second, and 1s 6d third. In this way the rigid class consciousness of the Victorians was perpetuated by the railway. Each class had its own level of comfort—and at larger stations their own waiting-rooms—according to the fare paid. While a smooth and smoke-free ride was beyond the dream of all, the first-class passenger had at least the comfort of padded seats and a fully enclosed carriage. But the poor third-class passenger was lucky if he even had a roof over his head. Stoppages were frequent, not to allow passengers to alight but for oiling and inspecting the engine. The hazards of rail travel were many and *Punch* was not being entirely frivolous when it advised all passengers to include in their luggage a copy of the *Railway Pocket Companion*. This was a finely-bound compendium containing 'a small bottle of water, a tumbler, a complete set of surgical instruments, a packet of lint, and directions for making a will'.

There was also a fourth (or 'Parliamentary') class on the Braintree to Maldon line. This arose from the Railways Act 1844 which made it compulsory for all companies to run at least one train a day at a fare of a penny a mile. So, for the poor who were fit enough to survive the rigours of Parliamentary class, the fare to Maldon was only 1s. The real breakthrough for the working classes, though, was the excursion. This made it possible for many to visit the seaside for the first time in their lives. The excursion trains were an extraordinary sight, stretching out for up to 25 or 30 carriages filled with as many as 1,200 passengers. They were occasions for great celebration, with bands playing and flags flying at the morning send-off. From Braintree there were regular summer excursions to Ipswich, Bury St Edmunds, and Norwich, and to the rapidly growing resorts of Walton, Lowestoft, and Great Yarmouth.

But the railway was more than a novelty, it was good business too. Several people wanted to extend the line beyond Braintree. In the late 1840s two extensions northwards were planned, first by the Braintree and Halstead Railway in 1846 and later by the Eastern Counties Railway to Saffron Walden in 1848. There were two further attempts, in 1856 and 1900, to revive the planned extension to Halstead, but these never got past the drawing-board. So, for a while, the Braintree line settled down to a fairly placid life. As traffic failed to develop as expected, the double track was reduced to a single line, the rails being sold to the War Office for use in Crimea. The planned level-crossing over the main line at Witham was never built, leaving two 'feeder' branches instead of a through line. Also, the proposed improvements to the harbour at Maldon were not carried out.

In 1860, though, an extension of the line westwards to Dunmow and Bishops Stortford was suggested. After a meeting at The Horn, the Bishops Stortford, Dunmow, and Braintree Railway Company was formed. In time they received permission to build the 18 mile line to Stortford and work began in 1864. Before it was finished the Company was absorbed into the Great Eastern Railway, which was created out of the amalgamation of the Eastern Counties Railway with other,smaller companies. Work on the line was slow, and the opening date was delayed several times. Only after the third inspection was the line passed as suitable for passenger traffic. The first train left Braintree at 7am on 22 February 1869 and arrived at Dunmow 35 minutes later. Its arrival was witnessed by 50 or 60 workmen on the bridge in the driving sleet. There were several visitors on the platform, but no ceremony. A regular passenger service of three trains a day was thus quietly introduced.

The railway changed lives, particularly for those living in villages close to the line. It opened up new horizons, offered the prospect of different jobs, and a different life. The exodus from the villages of Essex began with the railway, though it was accelerated after 1870 by changes in farming methods and an agricultural depression. In 1907 the *Victoria County History* observed: 'It has been said that only ''old people and fools'' are left in the villages. This exodus, which is chiefly to London, is depriving Essex villages of the most vigorous people'. But London was not the only magnet; each town on the railway attracted people from the nearby villages. The example of Braintree and Bocking makes this clear. Between 1841 and 1911, the population of Braintree increased from 3,670 to 6,168. In the same period, Bocking, which had no railway, grew only from 3,437 to 3,448.

The railway was a great stimulus to industry, attracting both heavy engineering and small workshop activity, making use of the goods carried on the Maldon to Braintree line. Before the railway there was only one coal merchant, Strutts of London Road, but soon after 1848 the coal trade grew. New merchants, some of them from Maldon, appeared in the town. By the end of the century there were eight, all occupying the goods yard in Railway Street. The easy transport and lower price of coal encouraged 140 local people to form a mutual coal club in 1851. They bought 180 tons of Durham and Northumberland coal at 18s a ton for distribution among their members. Although this particular scheme was short-lived, the railway increased the domestic use of coal, making Braintree homes both warmer and smokier.

The easier transport of lime, timber, slate, cement, bricks, and tiles encouraged house-building in the growing town. Building was mostly on the south-eastern side of the town, around the station and sidings. The area bounded by Coggeshall Road, Fairfield Road, South Street, and East Street was built on in the second half of the century. The town was undergoing major surgery. Before 1850 the surrounding fields reached to Market Square, and where Manor Street, Victoria Street, Fairfield Road, and Albert Road are now laid out, there were meadows delighting in such names as Cherry Orchard, Horse Fair Field, and Fair Field—the latter two a reminder of their part in the Braintree Fairs. Yet, by 1900, this area had become an urban factory and housing quarter.

The area was developed piecemeal by individual builders. The earlier houses were of timber and lath and plaster, then of cheap brick, and later of good red brick with decorative tiles, stone sills, and bay windows. This improvement is largely explained by the railway and the rise of builders' merchants in the town. By the middle of the 19th century these included: three brick and tile makers, six bricklayers, ten joiners and builders, nine painters, plumbers, and glaziers, and two timber merchants. A Brick and Tile Works stood just behind the station and was served by a private siding. The railway brought other improvements to life in the town. A Gas Works was built in New Street about 1840 and later was moved to Manor Street, where it could receive coal from the Goods Yard. Cheaper coal meant cheaper gas for both domestic use and street lighting. The railway also played a part in improving the town's drainage. Many of the cast-iron drain covers in the town still date from the 1860s, when they were made in Rayne. The foundry,of course, relied on the railway for transport of coal, pig-iron and castings.

The movement of agricultural foodstuffs and stock by railway helped to widen the area served by the Braintree market. Even after the new Corn Exchange in the High Street was opened in 1839, the corn trade had remained local with merchants coming from no further afield than Witham and Ware. The railway brought the market within the reach of London buyers, and trade became brisker. In 1858 the *Braintree Spectator* described the market 10 years after the arrival of the railway: 'the farmers and dealers riding and driving in from all quarters, quick upon each other's footsteps as the clock approaches the hour of twelve... the orderly row of desks where the samples are exposed and examined... we ourselves have seen the samples brought out again and large quantities of produce change hands as its owners were rapidly borne away'. By the middle of the century in Braintree, there were four corn factors, six corn millers, and 25 bakers and flour dealers.

The transport of barley and hops helped Braintree's brewing industry. Young's Brewery was in Railway Street, where the maltings still stand today. By the 1870s the brewery was equipped with steam plant, creating another advantage of being close to the Goods Yard where the coal merchants were. The other large brewing firm in the town, Ridleys, also sited their maltings close to the station, next to the Gas Works in Manor Street. These buildings, now used as a furniture depository, are still complete with chutes, hoppers, and perforated brick floors, and the initials 'TDR 1854' can still be seen on an adjoining house. In all there were three brewers and four maltsters in Braintree in 1848. They helped to keep the four coopers (barrel-makers) busy and the 30 hotels, inns, and taverns and 29 beerhouses well stocked. It is hardly surprising, in the face of these statistics, that the reputation of 'Braintree Beer' was known for miles around.

By the 1870s, cattle pens had been erected in the Goods Yard for the large numbers of animals carried by train. The railway also brought buyers from as far away as London and Taunton. It carried cattle from more distant parts than before—Scots, North and South Welsh, Herefords, Devons, and Shorthorns—and brought salesmen of modern agricultural machinery. But the railway also brought to an end the annual October Fair. In its heyday more than 20,000 sheep, as well as horses and cattle, were herded to the town by drovers. The railway so much speeded up transportation that from the 1870s the annual fair was replaced by weekly sales at Messrs Balls' saleyard in Market Lane, which was not so long ago demolished to make way for Tesco's supermarket.

The railway not only assisted established industries. By 1851, 19 men were employed in iron manufacture in the town. The transition from blacksmith to jobbing ironmonger to machine manufacturer occurred slowly at first, but accelerated towards the end of the century. In Bradford Street, Samuel Hawkes was listed as an 'iron founder and agricultural machine maker' in 1848. There was another works near Chapel Hill Farm, where threshing-machines were built. It was from small workshops like these that the large engineering firms which led Braintree's industrial growth in the 20th century grew.

So, both old and new benefitted from the railway. West's Brush Factory in Sandpit Lane, Adkins' Mat Manufactory, and Fullers, the Boot and Shoe Makers—these were just a few of the firms which profited from the wider market brought by the railway. Craftsmen and shopkeepers found a new briskness in Braintree's commercial life and the *Braintree Spectator* noted 'the alacrity with which the inmates and proprietors of the different shops in the early morning prepare for the business of the day'. Braintree had at last been invaded by 'railway time', and lost some of its older and more leisurely ways.

The Braintree Flyer. (ERO/JA)

ABOVE: Braintree station with footbridge to the Dunmow & Bishops Stortford platform. (ERO/JA) CENTRE: The Station, 1981, from the deserted Dunmow platform, and BELOW: the end of the line.

EASTERN COUNTIES' RAILWAY.

CHEAP TRIP
TO
LONDON.

On MONDAY, Aug. 13th, 1860,

JOHNSON'S
FIRST SPECIAL
EXCURSION TRAIN,
FOR THE SEASON,

Will leave Braintree Station at 6.30 a.m. calling at Witham at 6.50. a.m., returning from Bishopsgate Station at 8 p.m.

Giving ELEVEN HOURS IN LONDON.

FARES THERE & BACK,

FIRST CLASS. **5s.** COVERED CARRIAGES **2s.6d.**

Children, under 12 years of age half-price.

TICKETS may be had up to Saturday, the 11th Inst. of Mr. Finney, Bocking; Mr. Joseph Godfrey Downing, Chemist, Mr. Fred. Andrews, Grocer, and Mr. I. Clayden, Railway Tavern, Braintree; and Railway Stations, Witham and Braintree.

Any further Information may be had of the Contractor

Wm. JOHNSON, Railway Coal Depot.

Eastern Counties Railway.

A DAY AT THE GERMAN OCEAN!

EXCURSIONS
TO
HARWICH OR DOVERCOURT,

Affording an opportunity for a

TRIP ON THE RIVER ORWELL.

On MONDAY, JUNE 16th, and

EVERY MONDAY,

Until further notice, Passengers will be booked os under :—

FROM	Morning.	Fares to Harwich and Back. 1st Class. s.	d.	2nd Class. s.	d.	3rd Class. s.	d.
Stratford	7 45						
Ilford	7 59						
Romford	8 14	7	6	5	0	3	0
Brentwood	8 30						
Ingatestone	8 46						
Chelmsford	10 0						
Witham	10 20	6	6	4	0	3	0
Maldon	9 0						
Braintree	10 0						
Kelvedon	9 45						
Mark's Tey	10 35						
Chappel	9 40	4	6	2	9	2	0
Bures	9 30						
Sudbury	9 20						
Colchester	10 45	3	6	2	6	1	9
Ardleigh	10 35	3	0	2	0	1	6
Manningtree	11 5	2	6	1	3	1	0

Passengers by this Excursion can take **Boat Tickets** at 1s. each from Harwich to Ipswich, and return from either Town.

Tickets will not be transferable, and will be available for Return from Harwich or Ipswich, and to the issuing Station only, by Trains leaving Ipswich at 5.30 p.m.; and Harwich at 5.10 p.m. on the day of issue.

☞ Passengers by these Trains will not be allowed to carry Luggage.

Superintendent's Office,
Bishopsgate, June, 1856.

By Order.

PRINTED AT THE COMPANY'S WORKS, STRATFORD.

RIGHT: 'A day at the German Ocean', care of Eastern Counties Railway, 1856. (ERO/JA) LEFT: London excursion poster, 1860. (ERO/JA)

ABOVE: Station Approach, CENTRE: South Street, BELOW: West's Brush Factory staff. (ERO/JA)

A display of brushes from West's Brush Factory. (ERO/JA)

A Considerable Market

Oyster and mackerel sellers mingle with local farmers, corn merchants, millers, and brewers in the print of 'Braintree Market, 1826'. This scene—by Robert Crane, a popular painter of sporting scenes—is one of the best known from the town's past. Quite rightly so, too. For Braintree market is almost 800 years old and its story is the story of the town's growth from a huddled group of houses at the crossroads to a flourishing market town in the 19th century.

King John began it all c1199 when he granted Braintree a market charter. The colourful stalls packed tightly into the space which is now Little Square comprised the mediaeval market. Here farmers brought their animals and artisans their crafts to sell and barter with the townsmen and women. Agriculture was flourishing on the good arable soils, and as the farmers grew wealthy the market prospered. In 1594, the Essex historian Norden described the shire as 'most fatte, frutefulle, and full of profitable things'. As the stalls in the market-place multiplied, Braintree market began to burst at its seams.

Over the years, many of the stalls had been replaced by permanent structures, leaving only the narrowest of alleyways between them. These became a great obstruction to market users and a move to a more spacious site was long overdue. This move was heralded by the building of a new Market Cross in 1631. It was built in what became known as New Market Street—now simply New Street—to where the market was moved. The original Drury Lane Market Cross had by this time already fallen derelict. New Street began a new life as one of the busiest streets in the town.

Wagons and carts loaded with goods for the market bumped their way into town along this street. This was now the main road into the town from Maldon, the port through which Braintree's goods passed to and from London. With its new market and good communications Braintree was set to profit from the boom in Essex farming which marked the 1700s. By the start of the 18th century, the town pinned its hopes equally on the cloth trade and its market facilities. The annual cattle fair, too, proved so popular that in 1705 a second was granted by Queen Anne to the then lord of the manor, Herman Olmius.

One group of people who were glad to see the great numbers who came to Braintree on market-day and at fair-time, were the publicans. With more beer being swallowed each year, the town's inns became some of the most stable businesses. Several—such as The Horn and the Three Tuns—laid on a special meal for farmers on market-day. The inns became important meeting places; during the 17th century the Four and Twenty had met at either The Horn or The Cock (Bank Street). The White Hart in Bocking was the venue for turnpike business, while the shoemakers' union met at the Braintree White Hart. As well as providing drink, food, and a bed, the inns were also picking-up stages for coaches, stables for carriers, and the best places for commercial dealings. They were, in short, the very life-blood of the thriving market-town.

During the 18th century, the market began to replace the cloth trade as the source of the town's prosperity. By 1750 the Select Vestry, the town's social elite, included only three clothiers among its regular attenders. The jury list in 1768 showed just two clothiers. Yet the same list showed ten artisans, six innkeepers, and five shopkeepers. By 1783 the number of shopkeepers who were jurors was eight. The middle classes were profiting from the business which the market was attracting to the town. Master craftsmen, lawyers, corn merchants, auctioneers and wealthy farmers took root in Braintree. The makers of luxury items found a market here—like the Fordham family, clockmakers, who settled in the town for four generations. Builders also profited from the new spending power of the middling classes and farmers.

The growth of London was the chief stimulus to Essex farming. Better transport made it possible to send wheat quickly and cheaply to the London market. Another influence was the more progressive and scientific outlook of the farmers, in particular the large landowners. Men like Western of Rivenhall Place, Strutt of Terling Place, and Ruggles of Spains Hall, showed great interest in improving farmland. Many clothiers switched their energies and business sense from the cloth trade to farming, bringing a new spirit of enterprise to the time-honoured traditions of agriculture.

Profits were not the only incentive to landowners; estate improvement became a matter of duty and pride as well. The squire of Stisted Hall, Rev Charles Onley (who was in fact the Rector of Fordham, but who had gained the Hall and its estate by marriage) described this double satisfaction in this way: 'A field or two of perfectly hoed crops form, in the ramble, a necessary contrast to the grazing grounds, and, with good low hedges, a few clumps of plantation and a little water an ornamental farm is within the reach of every country gentleman, who may satisfy his honest pride and not injure (nay, probably improve) his fair income'. Onley was not unusual in these concerns, and, like several other local farmers, he was a contributor to Arthur Young's *Annals of Agriculture*.

The chief crop around Braintree was wheat, the output of which increased during the century. Hops too were grown, with some 60 acres devoted to them in Braintree and Bocking. Livestock was sacrificed to wheat, pasture being ploughed up in many places. Towards the end of the century the Norfolk four-course rotation (wheat, turnips, barley, and clover) was being used more and more. Clover flourished at Rayne, the Notleys, and Faulkbourne. Some efforts, though, were made with livestock. Arthur Young praised a Stisted farm as 'excellently adapted to a gentlemanly husbandry, that of making the arable land subservient to cattle'. Sheep too made an occasional appearance. 'Grazing is the farming of gentlemen', wrote Rev Onley, 'and that of sheep the most amusing and least hazardous'. The general picture, by the start of the 19th century, was, in the eyes of one traveller, of an 'opulent neighbourhood and well frequented market'. Such richness, he continues, was to be seen also at the town's fair which 'is noted for its hops, cheeses, butter, and beasts'.

Braintree's small population growth during the 18th century was due almost entirely to the fortunes of the market. The decline in the cloth trade had led to a drop in population of some 300 in the years from 1720 to 1780. But as the market industries took root, the final 20 years saw a rise from 2,400 to 2,821. At Bocking the picture was less healthy, and by 1800 the population was only 2,680, almost 500 less than in the 1720s. So, from being the larger of the two towns at the start of the century, Bocking fell behind Braintree, almost solely because Braintree had a market to fall back on when the cloth trade declined whereas Bocking did not. No longer were they seen as twin centres of cloth manufacture. In 1763, one observer wrote that 'in Bocking is a large manufactury of wool and is adjoining to Braintree a considerable market-town'. Today's prominence of Braintree over Bocking then is explained by the existence of Braintree market.

The first half of the 19th century was probably the golden age of the market. The story behind the commissioning of the market print in 1826 explains the commercial importance of the market. The general mood of confidence inspired the partners of the Sparrow Bank to commission the painting. What better subject matter, then, than the bank's most likely clients—the farmers. And what better setting than the market itself.

Details from the print suggest the general hubbub which arose from the market—a background of simmering conversation, interjected greetings, and the regular calls of street traders mixing with the barking of stray dogs and the startled whinnying of horses. Crammed into the High Street between the King's Head and The Horn are farmers, millers, corn-merchants and others from places as far afield as Thaxted, Halstead or Colchester. Each week they come to conduct their business and pay their respects at the bars of the town's pubs. The constant circling of farmers from one knot of gossiping and bargaining to another made Robert Crane's task a difficult one. Being a most thorough artist he overcame this by spending several weeks making water-colour sketches of the people he wanted in the picture as they sat in their own home. Only then did he transfer the personal details onto the larger scene. As a result of this it is possible to recognise several local characters.

On the far left is the rotund figure of Abraham Medcalf, a Braintree butcher and cattle dealer, chatting to Captain Peers of Rayne. Near to them, and drowning their conversation with his bell, is Ben, the waiter at The Horn, who is advertising the farmer's 'ordinary' or cheap meal. Moving across the street, our gaze flickers past a group of farmers from Black Notley, Finchingfield, and Wethersfield, and alights on the smart figure of John English Tabor of 'Fennes', Bocking. He is wearing the blue swallow-tail coat, knee-breeches, and leather boots favoured by the wealthier farmers of the day. He is in animated conversation—perhaps about some proposed new buildings for his farm—with Thomas Franklin, the Thaxted surveyor, who is wearing a billycock hat and white smock.

The central figure, standing alone, is Samuel Bright of Braintree. He was a prominent farmer, maltster, brewer, and wine-merchant, who owned a shop in High Street. On the extreme right are two of the town's characters, in comic contrast with each other. Slightly to the fore is the bearish shape of great John Digby who could be heard 'hollering mackerel' as far away as Coggeshall. Dwarfed by Digby, though of equal fame, is the diminutive William Finch, tailor, 'the only man in Essex who could cut a pair of breeches'. One notable landmark of the street which is missing is the Corn Exchange. This was not built until 1839, but from then, its four pillar portico and prominent clock added a touch of grandeur to the street and the dealings of the market.

Animal pens were laid out on the Fair Field and in Great Square right up to the present century. The weekly cattle market had largely moved into Messrs Balls' saleyards at the back of New Street by this time. Here, until quite recently, townspeople gathered to buy goats, chickens, and ducks, to cast an eye over the farmers' stock, and simply to chat. It was here you caught up with the town gossip—at a time when everyone knew everyone else—and where children stared with a mixture of fear and excitement as the cowmen smacked their heavy sticks on the animals' hide. These are the memories shared by those who knew Braintree before the cattle market was pulled down to make way for Tesco's supermarket. Now the only animals present are the plastic-wrapped joints on the butcher's counter. About the same time the Corn Exchange too was demolished. The memory of the market was dealt a double blow.

Of course, the market had long since fallen from its great days at the middle of the 19th century. Essex farming had passed through a boom period in the 1850s and 1860s with a growing urban population making greater demands for food. But a corresponding down-turn was on its way. This worsened into a severe depression after 1874. A run of disastrous harvests and, above all, the import of cheap American wheat brought ruin to many Essex farms, especially in the arable areas. This depression meant a decline in the market and a threat to the town's livelihood. It would have to change its character if it was to survive. This was a turning point; when the 20th century arrived the market-town had died and Braintree was emerging as an industrial centre. Today only the weekly fruit and vegetable market survives—a relic of an 800 year tradition.

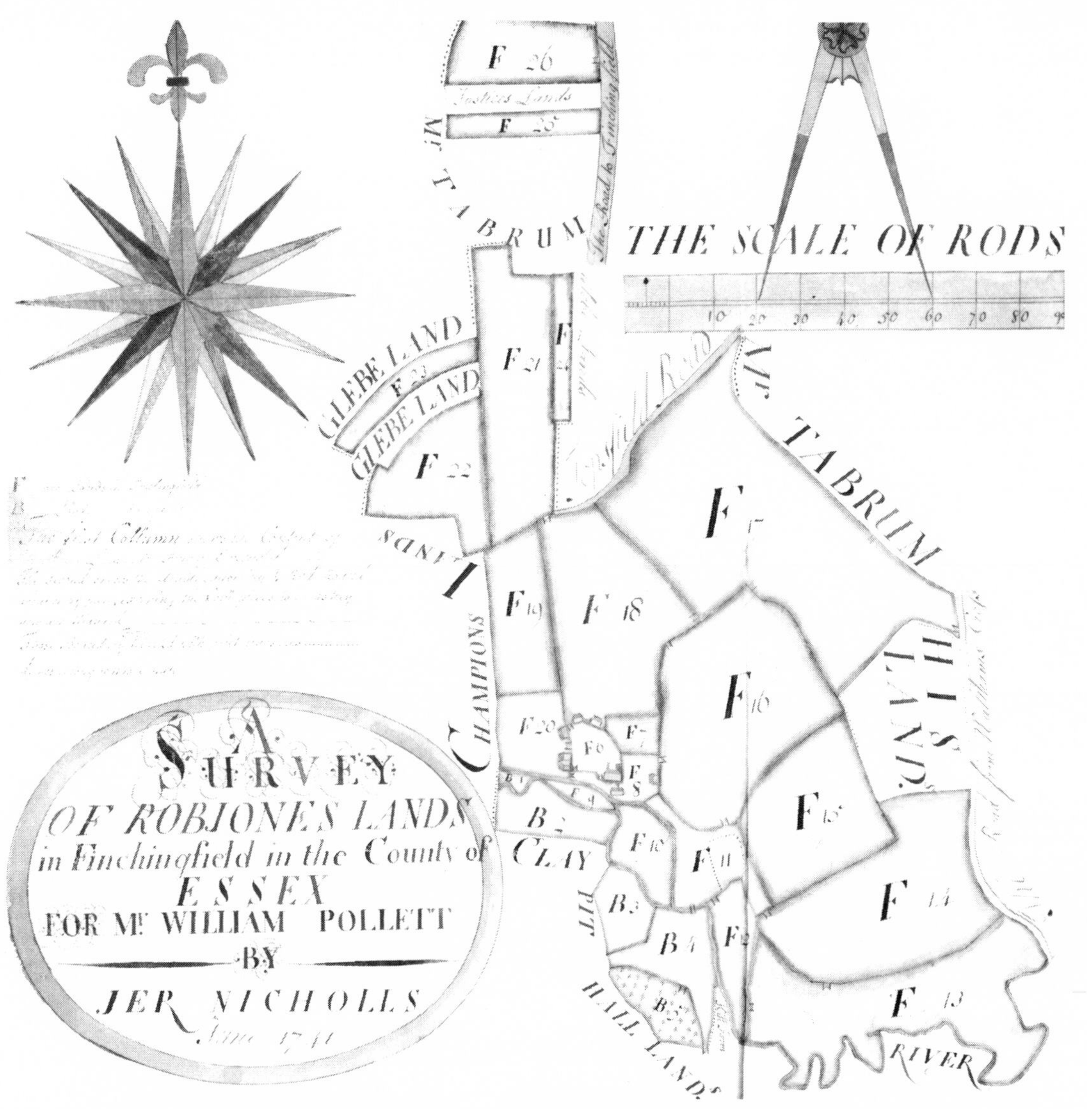

Part of a survey of 1741 of Finchingfield Farmland. (CB)

KEY

1	Little Britain	14	Broom Ley
2	Bardfield Mead	15	New Field
3	,,	16	Eight Acres
4	,,	17	Sedmans
5	Launders Piece In Bardfield	18	Home Field
		19	Sandy Piece
6	Cow Yard etc.	20	Cow House Field
7	Orchard	21	Five Acres in the Great Common
8	Backhouse Yard	22	Stone Piece
9	Horse Watering	23	Sandy Piece
10	Round Meadow	24	Little Piece
11	Home Meadow	25	In the Middle Common
12	Little Meadow	26	,,
13	Long Meadow		

TOTAL OF 88 ACRES

ABOVE and CENTRE: Harvesting in fields near Braintree. (NG) BELOW: Braintree from near Notley Road. (ERO/JA)

ABOVE: Stisted Hall, 1832, and BELOW: the Hall and Church, 1820. (NG)

ABOVE: The Onley Arms, Stisted. (NG) CENTRE: Animal pens on the site of the Town Hall, Market Square. (NG) BELOW: Market Square and Nag's Head, c1900. Far left, the Orange Tree Inn. (ERO/JA)

Schools and Entertainment

The Braintree Grammar School was one of the earliest in Essex. Sadly it was also one of the most short-lived. Yet it produced at least one scholar of world eminence—John Ray, the naturalist. Ray was born in 1627 and was the third and youngest child of a Black Notley blacksmith. The family lived in a six-room cottage of timber and plaster, which still stands in Bakers Lane. After village school in Black Notley, it was decided that the bright ten year old should continue his studies at Braintree Grammar School. So each day, John Ray walked down the Notley Road into Braintree to St Michael's Church which housed the schoolroom. Here he came to the attention of the vicar and schoolmaster Samuel Collins. With the vicar's help, Ray won a place at Cambridge University when he was 17. The money to enable him to go came from a scholarship arising from Braintree rents, for which the vicar was the sole trustee.

After a brilliant Cambridge career, Ray was elected a minor fellow at Trinity in 1649. There he lectured in Greek, Mathematics, and Humanities. But, as another in the tradition of Braintree dissenters, he refused to sign the Act of Uniformity (which prescribed the use of the Book of Common Prayer in the Church of England). This cost him his academic career at the university. Luckily a wealthy former pupil of his, Francis Willoughby, came to his aid. Together they travelled the British Isles on horseback, noting and recording all the plant types they came across. Their travels were, in effect, the first thorough botanical survey ever carried out in Britain.

This field-work prompted two major scientific works—*Historia Plantarum* (1686) and *Catalogus plantarum Angliae* (1670)—which earned him a reputation as the father of English natural history. His most well-known and influential book, though, was *The Wisdom of God manifested in the Works of Creation* (1691). This deeply affected 18th century philosophy and brought attention to the physical world of nature which was thought to provide a guide to the right behaviour of man. Ray's work was at the very start of a movement which created the 18th century taste for the countryside. His influence extended to the writings of Shaftesbury on the importance of the visible world upon the way the mind worked, to the taste for 'rural retirement' among poets like Pope, and to the reverence for nature in Romantic poetry.

Ray returned to Black Notley in his later years. Two of his companions at this time were Benjamin Allen (1663-1738) and Samuel Dale (1659-1738). Allen was a physician and amateur naturalist. He ran his practice from his home, the 'Great House' in Great

Square, where he also wrote two major books on springs and mineral waters. Dale, a prominent member of the 'Four and Twenty' in the later years of that august company, also took a keen interest in botany. He ran his doctor's practice from Bocking End—from the building which is now the home of the solicitors Holmes and Hills—until his death at the age of 80. He wrote *The History of Harwich* and several learned medical works. Finally, another notable Braintree doctor of the 17th century was Samuel Collins, son of the Braintree vicar who taught Ray, who served for nine years as chief physician to Peter the Great, the Tsar of Russia. He died in 1670 in Paris, on his way home from treating the Tsar. A bronze memorial to him is placed in the east end of St Michael's, just above the grave of his father.

Despite its famous son, the Braintree Grammar School was closed in the middle of the 17th century. It has never been revived. During the next century, the only education for ordinary children was provided by the Charity Schools. The earliest in Braintree was endowed by James Coker, a grocer. He died in 1702 and left all his lands in trust to pay for the teaching of 10 poor children of the parish in English and Latin. By the early 19th century, the income of the trust was applied to the British School. This had been set up by the British Schools Society which, along with the National Schools Society, launched a campaign in 1810 aimed at universal education.

These two societies were strongly supported by Dissenters, and in Braintree notably by the Courtaulds. The British School was in Martin's Yard and was run by the vicar of St Michael's, Rev Bernard Scalé. From 1820, there was a second British School, this one in Manor Street. In 1850 an attempt was made to re-open the Coker Charity School. A schoolroom was set up at the back of what is now Townrow's shop in Bank Street. Ten boys, named 'Coker's Scholars', were to be taught the three R's and 'the rudiments of Latin grammar as far as it is conducive to a more correct knowledge of the English tongue, and a strict inculcation of religious principles in accordance with the doctrine and discipline of the Church of England'. Other children were admitted for fees ranging from 4d to 6d a week. The school did not last long and closed in 1853.

Another British School was opened at Bocking End in 1852. This had its origins in the Charity School founded by the Bocking Independent Congregation next to the chapel at Bocking End. In 1747, 39 members of the Congregation had subscribed £40 19s for a boys' school. The three R's were once again the basics of the curriculum. The master was required to be of good character and qualified to teach Latin and Greek. His salary was £30 a year. In the 1760s, girls too were admitted, and by 1812 there were 80 boys and 32 girls at the school. Teaching was on the Lancastrian plan, with the oldest pupils acting as monitors, passing on what they had learnt to the younger children.

There were also private establishments for the sons and daughters of those who could afford to pay the fees. In 1851, there were four such schools, all taking boarders. There was Sarah Boosey's seminary in Bradford Street and Elizah Beuzeville's school. The other two were on London Road, being Alex Hart's Academy for Boys and Catherine Hart's School for Ladies. The schools were big enough for Mr Hart to need an assistant teacher, while Mrs Hart employed 'a teacher of wax flowers' and 'a teacher of drawing'. Both of these households included a cook and a maid, who helped to see that the offspring of the farmers and tradesmen lived in the manner to which they were accustomed. The large Public Schools, like Felsted, remained the preserve of the gentry.

Manor Street School, the oldest of Braintree's present schools, was built in 1863 on the site of the old British School. After the 1870 Education Act—which laid the foundation of the modern education system—a local school board was set up and could compel school attendance to the age of 13. In 1875 the Manor Street School was run by the Braintree School Board. Before then, the standard of teaching at the school varied enormously. Official inspection was a condition of state grants, and these would be cut if the reports were unsatisfactory. The school's logbook reveals the fear that preceded the inspector's visit. One of the best known inspectors was Mathew Arnold, the great Victorian poet and son of Thomas Arnold, the headmaster of Rugby School. Mathew Arnold's signature appears several times on the Manor Street School reports.

The school day ran from 8.55 am to 4 pm, with a break for lunch. During the 1860s there were about 180 children on the register, but truancy was common and attendance was usually around 150. The annual summer treat took place in the grounds of George Courtauld's house to which the pupils, headed by the Rifle Corps Band, paraded through the streets. Half days were granted for the County Agricultural Show and for Braintree's October Cattle Fair.

The Braintree Fairs had been entertaining the people of Braintree for centuries. They were one of the few amusements available to working people, who had little time or money to spend on leisure. But for the really wealthy, those who lived at Stisted Hall or Gosfield Hall, the culture of Europe was available. The greater ease of travel brought both Europe and London within reach of the local aristocracy and gentry in the 18th century. Characteristic of the frivolous, sophisticated county set was Earl Nugent of Gosfield Hall. He made his money by marrying rich widows—from which activity Walpole coined a new verb 'to nugentise'. His second wife left him the Hall. In line with the 18th century taste for architecture and landscape gardening, he devoted his energies to turning the 16th century Hall into a residence suitable for an 18th century gentleman. He remodelled the south front in a classical style and embellished the north with giant Corinthian pilasters. His masterpiece, though, was the creation of the splendid mile-long lake. For the finishing touch, he had his portrait painted by Gainsborough.

The lesser gentry lived well too, though confined their pleasures nearer home. Braintree never became a sophisticated, fashionable centre, but there were several towns close by which did. Braintree's wealthier tradesmen could visit the Strawberrry Gardens at Sible Hedingham and the theatres at Chelmsford, Colchester, or Castle Hedingham. Nearby Witham was a well-known spa, owing its success to a Dr Taverner who rediscovered a spring which had earlier been found to possess medicinal qualities. In 1737 he wrote a pamphlet trumpeting the presence of sulphur in the water. As the Essex gentry rushed to 'take the waters', Witham's inns and lodging-houses profited, and other entertainments were spawned.

The spas played on the 18th century concern with health. Like the country's seaside resorts, they mostly date from the second half of the century. The notebook of Joseph and John Savill reveals that Braintree's well-to-do travelled both England and Europe for their health's sake:

'June 1776 — Mrs Thomas Ruggles was brot through town and carried to Clare to be buryed. She died at Lisbon—whent there for the recovery of her health and died.

Sep 1795 — Mother, Sister Walker, and Miss Walker, and myself whent to view Southend.

Sep 1804 — My wife and self whent to Buxton to bathe.

Nov 1818 — My wife and I set off for Bath, Brighton, Cheltenham, and Malvern for the benefit of change of air...I was extremely unwell at times during our absence of 24 weeks'.

Travel for its own sake also became popular for the first time. A wealth of travel literature was published. But a 'tour' was, above all, something to do rather than read about. One Braintree man who went on, and wrote about tours of the countryside was John Cunnington. Between 1790 and 1800 he travelled throughout Essex on horseback, sketching churches and making architectural and historical notes. A fascinating account of the different crossings over the river Crouch is just one of his many descriptions of the county:

'Sep 1799—Crossing the Crouch.

1. By the Cricksey Ferry, near Burnham—a good horse ferry but bad for a carriage, when the wind is strong there is much danger of being aground.
2. By the Grambridge Ferry—indifferent for horses and very bad for carriages.
3. By Hull Bridge—the river may be forded here about one hour and a half before and after low water.
4. At Battle Bridge—here is a good new wooden bridge'.

Cunnington is an example of the well-to-do, urbane 18th century gentleman. His diary is filled with thoughts upon the French Revolution, extracts from Laurence Sterne's letters, and notes upon various Essex 'oddities'. Of the latter, two at least are worth quoting here: '...a whalebone on the road to Chelmsford, near the ten-mile stone, from a whale taken in the Thames in 1685'; '...Hadley Green, a neat modern house built by Lady Donhoff about 1796—this lady, daughter of the third Earl of Tankerville, name of Camilla Elizabeth, had been intimately connected with the late King of Poland'.

Of course, only a few Braintree people had the leisure to travel about the country for pleasure. Yet there were enough to support the town's coffee-house and bookshop. Luxuries were plentiful for this class of Braintree society. When they were married they might have—as did Andrew Fuller and Betty English in 1770—a wedding dinner of 'two legg of mutton and two puddings'. Or, less happily, at their funeral they might have—like Richard Reece in 1757—six 'Paull Bearers', each wearing 'a hatband, scarf, and ring' bought specially for the occasion.

Their houses too were well stocked and provided, on occasion, rich pickings for burglars. John Savill discovered this to his cost one March night in 1822: 'On Sunday night the shutters of my kitchen windows were forced open, an aperture made in the window and entered by one or two persons at least. Several doors were opened by forcing the bolts, every drawer ransacked and left open in the kitchen and scullery without taking any articles out. My loss consisted of four common spoons, a valuable tea-pot stand, a tinder box, part of a roasted leg of pork and a piece of cheese. My plate was saved in the store room, I believe due to a strong wind at the time blowing a door to very smartly which alarmed the family and the thieves made off'.

Most people, though, had little time for leisure or money for anything more than the bare essentials. When they did take to amusements, it was usually in a full-blooded way. This often centred around the inn or ale-house, where cock-fighting and card-playing were diversions to the main business of drinking beer. Gambling, of course, added an extra spice. Braintree's two fairs were the high points in the entertainment calendar. There were also special occasions such as the Coronation or, as in 1784, 'celebrations of general peace' with 'illuminations and fireworks'.

Central to all these entertainments was the much-famed 'Brayntry Beer'. There were several brewers in the town, so the topic of which was the best brew demanded a great deal of attention. So much so, that the town's 19th century historian devoted several pages of his history to the subject of Braintree's beer. As today, pundits like Cunnington thought yesterday's beer better than today's. Talking of the sociability of the townspeople, he says 'there used to be until lately plenty of good beer to induce them to it'.

He then described how stout 'Braintreeonians' set about finding the best pint in town: '...they used to find out where the best beer was and there they used to resort every morning at 11 am to take their usual draught of the ale together; and there used to be considerable rivalry amongst the publicans as to who should be honoured with the company of these connoisseurs in beer, in order to obtain which they often volunteered a cold ham and some hot drop-dumplings. And at these meetings would arise the important question "Is not the beverage perfect?" which would sometimes be answered in negative in consequence of some nice distinction as this: "It looks well in the glass, its brightness and frothing are excellent, it palates well—but it is rather bitter at the finish, namely at the smack of the mouth after it has been swallowed" '.

As the 19th century progressed there began to be a little more organised leisure for working people. In 1864 the Literary and Mechanics Institute, now called simply the

'Institute', was opened by its benefactor George Courtauld. Here working men could attend lectures, borrow books, and read the London papers. There was a Braintree Bicycle Club, which staged an annual race from Bay Tree Farm on the Coggeshall road to the County Courthouse (now the Public Library). Competitors were handicapped according to the size of their wheels. A football club was run from West's Brush Factory and their results were probably carried in the *Braintree & Bocking Advertiser* which began circulation in 1859. There was no regular theatre or music-hall, but the great Shakespearean actor, Edmund Kean, appeared early in the century with a company of strolling players in a New Street barn.

Yet in leisure, as in most things, the wealthy and the poor remained apart. A member of the gentry—such as Mr Tabor who held at various times Blake End Farm and Pattiswick Farm—rode with the East Essex Foxhounds and gambled at cards at least once a week. He was also in the Braintree Book Society, which was founded in 1802 and claimed to be the oldest book society in the country when it was still running in the 1960s. The Society's annual dinner, held in the Reading Room of the Horn, cost Mr Tabor 16s. It must have been a lavish affair. So too was the Bocking Ball, for which Mr Tabor bought a pair of white kid-gloves for 3s and had a 6d haircut.

For a glimpse of life further up the social scale, we need look no further than the list of Major Gepp's kit for the Loyal Chelmsford Volunteers' camp at Braintree in 1804. There are 80 items in all, including such absolute necessities as: a toasting fork; a pair of silver sugar tongs; ten pairs of stockings; six waistcoats (two ordinary, two regimental, and two coloured); a backgammon table and chess set; a cribbage board and cards; and a flute. Mind you, he was going away for a whole 15 days. The Officers' Mess was at the Horn, where they held three parties and a dance and dined on the few evenings when they were not eating at the tables of the local aristocracy. In the mornings they rested by watching their soldiers doing marching drill.

LEFT: John Ray of Black Notley. (ERO/JA) RIGHT: 'Dewlands', Black Notley: John Ray's home. BELOW: John Ray's pyramidal tomb in Black Notley churchyard. The altar-shaped tomb is Dr Benjamin Allen's (1663-1738).

ABOVE LEFT: Dr Samuel Dale (1659-1738) of Bocking End. (ERO/JA) RIGHT: Constitutional Club, 1981. LEFT: Rear of Great House, Great Square: home of Dr Benjamin Allen. (ERO/JA) RIGHT: Great House c1890, and BELOW: c1900 (NG).

ABOVE: Braintree National School group. (NG) BELOW: Finchingfield School group. (NG).

ABOVE: Manor Street School group, 1917. (NG) RIGHT: Bradwell School group, 1919. (NG). BELOW LEFT: Infants School, Manor Street. RIGHT: Manor Street School, 1981.

ABOVE: Braintree Senior School, Panfield Lane before the official opening, October 1938. (JA) CENTRE: Main hall, Senior School. (JA) BELOW: Gosfield Lake and Hall, c1900. (ERO/JA).

The Braintree & Bocking Advertiser

ADVERTISEMENTS AND COMMUNICATIONS FOR THE EDITOR OR PUBLISHERS SHOULD BE FORWARDED TO THE OFFICE, HIGH STREET, BRAINTREE.

No. 1,062. WEDNESDAY, MARCH 3, 1880.

KING'S UNRIVALLED STOCKS OF FARM SEEDS.

MANGEL, SWEDE, TURNIP, AND CABBAGE,

JOHN K. KING,

SEED GROWER, COGGESHALL, ESSEX.

TO FARMERS.

R. TRIBBLE,

SADDLER AND HARNESS MAKER,

GREAT SQUARE, BRAINTREE,

NEW SADDLERY AND HARNESS.

THE RAILWAY COAL DEPOT, BRAINTREE.

W. JOHNSON AND SON,

MERCHANTS AND CONTRACTORS

COALS,

GIBBS' PURE FEEDING CAKE,

J. BRUNNING,

WOOLLEN DRAPER, TAILOR, AND HATTER,

BANK STREET, BRAINTREE.

J. BRUNNING,

WOOLLEN DRAPER, TAILOR, HATTER, AND GENERAL OUTFITTER,

BANK STREET, BRAINTREE.

JOHN GROVES,

COAL, LIME, & SLATE MERCHANT

I. BELSHAM AND SON,

COAL, OILCAKE, & MANURE MERCHANTS,

BRAINTREE.

AGRICULTURAL SALT.

DISSOLVED GUANO AND ARTIFICIAL MANURES.

COAL! COAL! COAL

A. WALFORD AND CO.

BEST DESCRIPTIONS OF HOUSE AND STEAM COALS,

UPPER RAILWAY STREET, BRAINTREE.

EDWARD BLOOMFIELD,

FURNISHING & GENERAL IRONMONGER,

HIGH STREET, BRAINTREE.

PATENT TRIPLE ACTION EXTINGUISHER LAMP.

WROUGHT IRON HURDLES AND FENCING.

SOLE AGENT FOR BRAINTREE

THE CASH SYSTEM.

CHARLES TOWNROW

THE MODERN SYSTEM

CASH PAYMENTS,

READY-MONEY ONLY!!!

CHARLES TOWNROW

WOOLLENS

READY-MONEY BASIS.

JUVENILE FANCY SUITS,

CHARLES TOWNROW,

CASH TAILOR, HATTER, CLOTHIER,

GENERAL OUTFITTER,

65, HIGH STREET, BRAINTREE.

DENTAL NOTICE.

MR. CHARLES SKIPP,

JOSCELYNE BROS.,

IRON BEDSTEADS AT OLD PRICES.

62, HIGH STREET, BRAINTREE.

BARNARD & LAKE,

RAYNE FOUNDRY, BRAINTREE ESSEX

IMPLEMENTS OF ANY MAKER AT CATALOGUE PRICES.

CHARLES BRASIER,

BRAINTREE.

BOOTS! BOOTS!! BOOTS!!!

FULLER'S

GREAT ANNUAL SALE

STRONG HOME-MADE BOOTS

WILL BE CONTINUED FOR A FEW DAYS LONGER

A FEW HUNDRED PAIRS WILL BE SOLD REGARDLESS OF COST,

COME EARLY!

RICHARD CRITTALL,

WHOLESALE AND RETAIL

FURNISHING & GENERAL IRONMONGER

BANK STREET, BRAINTREE,

BATH AND RANGE WORK.

GASFITTING AND BELLHANGING, ELECTRIC AND PNEUMATIC BELLS FIXED.

J. BENSON,

PLUMBER, GLAZIER, GENERAL HOUSE DECORATOR

94, HIGH STREET, BRAINTREE

PAPER HANGINGS,

MANUFACTURERS BY SPECIAL WARRANT TO THE QUEEN

COLMAN'S MUSTARD

CHINA, GLASS, AND EARTHENWARE.

G. T. BARTRAM,

BANK STREET, BRAINTREE

PRICE ONE PENNY.

BRAINTREE & BOCKING

. . Eighth Annual . .

FETE & RACES

HELD ON THE

Fete Field, Panfield Lane, Bocking,

Bank Holiday, August 3rd, 1908.

The Ground will be opened at 1.30 o'clock.

COMMITTEE:

President: G. T. BARTRAM, Esq., J.P., C.C.

Vice-Presidents: GUY GOLD, Esq. R. J. JOHNSON, Esq.

Treasurer: Mr. L. J. ALDEN.

Mr. A. J. Bagley	Mr. A. French	Mr. C. H. Howard	Mr. C. O. Rankin
,, W. Baldwin	,, H. W. Fuller	,, G. Hunnable	,, H. J. Rees
,, W. Beard	,, J. Fuller	,, E. Ingold	,, A. L. Saunders
,, C. F. Blanks	,, G. A. Gage	,, W. B. Kilroy	,, P. R. Stevens
,, C. A. Brown	,, G. Gibson	,, C. King	,, A. Stubbs
,, H. C. Brown	,, F. J. Green	,, W. Mayhew	,, J. Sydes
,, W. Clark	,, A. Harrington	,, G. Osborn	,, W. H. Tilston
,, B. W. Cornell	,, T. Harrington	,, A. Parchment	,, W. Vale
,, R. S. Crickmore	,, J. Harrison	,, W. Parmenter	,, J. B. Young
,, W. H. Dyson	,, P. V. Hawkes	,, J. Perry	
,, C. Edwards	,, G. W. Hicks	,, G. Phipps	

FRED. J. FULLER, Secretary.

ADMISSION: On the Day, 1/-; Children under 12, 6d.

Tickets at Half-Price if purchased on or before Aug. 1st.

RAILWAY ARRANGEMENTS:

Special Late Trains will leave Braintree as follows—

For Rayne, Felstead, Dunmow, Takeley, Bishop Stortford, and London ... ... } 8.45 P.M.

For Bulford, White Notley, Witham, Chelmsford, Brentwood, and London; Maldon, Kelvedon, Marks Tey, and Colchester ... ... } 9.30 P.M.

P. V. Hawkes, Printer, Braintree

LEFT: The *Braintree & Bocking Advertiser,* 3 March 1880. (JA) RIGHT: Programme for annual fete and races, 1908. (ERO/JA)

Entertainment bill
from
The Essex Newsman, 1907

HELLO! HELLO!

THE BOCKING MINSTRELS.

THIS POPULAR COMPANY will give an ENTERTAINMENT in the HALL of the MECHANICS' INSTITUTE, BRAINTREE, on THURSDAY NEXT, April 11.

GOOD BAND. GOOD TROUPE.
GOOD SINGING. . . GOOD JOKES.

NO VULGARITY. SEE BILLS.

DON'T FORGET APRIL 11.

ABOVE: Literary & Mechanics Institute, Bocking End, c1900. (ERO/JA)
BELOW: The Institute, 1981.

ABOVE: Braintree 'Cycling Club at Saling Grove, 1904. (ERO/JA) CENTRE: Weavers' Annual Walking Race from Bethnal Green to Braintree, 1901. The winner was No 3, Harry Spinks. (WA) BELOW: Workmen's Hall, Church Street, Bocking c1900.

A Walk In Yesterday's Town

It is early evening on 30 March 1851. Henry Jackson has just locked up his solicitor's office and walked to his home in Rayne Road. As he comes through the door he is welcomed by his wife Maria and his nine year-old son Henry. Their footman, James, is standing by to take Mr Jackson's hat and coat, while Elizabeth, the housemaid, is setting the dinner table. Downstairs in the kitchen, Charlotte, the cook, is putting the joint of beef onto a plate.

Just a few hundred yards away, in Boar's Head Yard, Ann Prentice has nearly finished her last load of washing for the day. She is 59 and a widow. She has to take in washing to support her family. Her 17-year-old son, Francis, helps with the wages he brings home as an apprentice coach spring smith. But this is not enough, for there is her grandson, four-year-old James, to look after. That is why Ann's daughter Emily is not yet back from her shift at the Silk Factory. Emily is ten.

These are just two glimpses of life in Braintree at the time of the 1851 Census. With the help of this record, it is possible to take an imaginary walk through the town. Starting at the corner of Rayne Road and Bank Street, we find the present Barclays Bank bearing the name of Sparrow Bank & Co in large letters. The bank manager, Hyem Porter, is out of town, but his wife and three children are at home. The rest of the household includes a sister-in-law, two bank clerks, a school governess, and three servants.

The Sparrow Bank was established in the town in 1803 and was one of the few which survived the 'panic' of 1825-6, during which some 70 or 80 English banks came to grief. It did not survive without a scare though. In 1826, the bank was forced, by a shortage of funds, to suspend payment. The story goes that there was then a 'run' on the bank, which was only averted by Thomas Nottidge, a wealthy farmer, who ostentatiously deposited two bags of gold there. Confidence soon returned and the bank continued until 1896 when it was absorbed by Barclay & Co.

Across Rayne Road, and strictly speaking in the parish of Bocking, is a fine house, with railings along the street front, where the English family lived. Somewhere behind the house was the English farm and the barn where John Bunyan is said to have preached while staying with the family. The railings were removed within living memory and the house has been renamed Electricity House. Back on the Braintree side of Rayne Road, we pass in turn the homes of: Samuel Bennett, a Master Grocer;

John Last, a hardwaresman; Frederick Smoothy, an attorney; Abraham Garrard, a veterinary surgeon; and Martha Pask, a widow and 'Independent Landed Proprietor'. Finally, at the junction with Sandford Pond Lane, is the silk factory of George Vavasseur.

Once round the corner into Sandford Pond Lane—now Sandpit Lane—we enter an area inhabited by tradesmen and master craftsmen. On a weekday this lane is filled with the sounds of hammers and saws from the many small workshops. Here are shoemakers, brushmakers, a wheelwright, a whitesmith, a trunkmaker, dressmakers, seamstresses, and others. Yet, here we find, between a butcher and a journeyman ironmonger, a 'professor of languages' and his wife, also a teacher of French. They may well have taught in one of the London Road academies or perhaps taught the aspiring sons and daughters of the town's wealthier tradesmen in their own homes.

Moving on to the junction with High Street—in what is now known as Brand's Yard—is John West's brush and pattens factory. West employed 43 men, 16 women, and 12 boys in his workshops. Further round the corner is a group of buildings owned by Sarah and Elizabeth Joscelyne. They rented the shop and house there to Thomas Archer, a clothier and hatter. This was one of the smartest shops in town, for Archer employed three assistants and a porter. From here we can see the sign of the Boar's Head, one of the oldest pubs in town. The tiny cottages huddled around the inn's yard mostly house workers at the brush factory or the silk factory in Martin's Yard.

A few yards further on is another pub which still flourishes today—The Wheatsheaf. William Cook and his wife Mary pull the pints here and are helped by a cook, a maid, a pot-boy, and an ostler. The view from the pub across to the church would be unrecognisable today. For where the fountain now stands, there was a row of houses, among which was the Prince of Wales, one of many Braintree pubs to have vanished over the years. On the other side of St Michael's Road, where the convent now stands, is the Maltings owned by Thomas Chalk. An engraving of the town, as seen from Notley Road, shows the oast-house standing out clearly against the backdrop of trees which at that time grew thickly in the churchyard.

Returning to the town centre by the High Street we pass, sandwiched between the Corn Exchange and the Falcon inn, the shop of James Joscelyne, Printer and Bookseller. The better known branch of the Joscelyne family business was not here, though, but at the corner of High Street with New Street. Few family businesses can boast continuous occupation of the same premises since the 18th century. Yet, as early as 1778, Benjamin Joscelyne was working for John Barritt, a cabinet-maker, at 62 High Street, the former White Hart Inn. In 1791, Benjamin took over the business. He and his wife Mary had 15 children in all, thus making sure that there was plenty of family to carry on the business.

When Benjamin died in 1839, his eldest son John took over. By 1851, he had diversified and gave his occupation as 'Auctioneer and Upholsterer'. Among his four children were Henry, who later took over the business, and Clement, who started the independent Joscelyne firm at Bishops Stortford. At this time the shop extended over just a small part of the present premises. Having already moved into one of the town's ancient hostelries, Joscelyne's further expansion took in more pubs. An old print of New Street shows the signs of the Three Tuns, The George and Dragon, and The Green Man. These pubs, which stood in a row, were known respectively as Little Hell, Great Hell, and Damnation from the scenes of drunkenness common there. Henry Joscelyne bought out these pubs one by one until he owned premises stretching down New Street as far as Market Lane. The 17th century staircase which once led to the ball room of the Three Tuns can still be seen in the shop. Joscelyne's history is a fine example of one of the town's many long-lived family businesses which, taken together, provide a large slice of the story of Braintree.

Emerging from Joscelyne's, and looking across the open space of Great Square, we see one of the finest houses in the 19th century town—'The Great House' (now the Constitutional Club). Behind its Georgian seven-bay front lived John Oates Harrison, a successful currier and leather cutter. He died in 1901, at the age of 91, and was buried in the graveyard of the Friend's Meeting House in Rayne Road. From Great Square we turn into Drury Lane, where silk workers, labourers, and paupers lived in the cottages standing between the lane and 'Cherry Orchard' field (now Blyth's Meadow car park).

Passing through Little Square, we come to Bank Street which has a very different look to it from today. Two 'islands' divide the street; the first was Dr Harrison's garden, and the second was occupied by two houses. These islands were a great nuisance to traffic, and there were plans to remove them as early as the 18th century. Yet they survived until the last war, and many people can still remember when W. F. Parkes & Son and the tailors, Pluck & Collins, had shops on the second one. Dr Harrison's garden stood between the ancient Swan Inn and the doctor's house which stood on the site of the present Woolworths. His eight-bedroom house had been the George Inn, a 16th century building with a traditional central gateway and courtyard. Like another 16th century pub, the Falcon in the High Street, this is one of Braintree's long forgotten inns.

Next to the Harrison home is the site of one of the country's oldest ironmonger's shops. John Batty first began his ironmonger's business there in 1639, and he was followed by others of the same trade until, in 1864, the shop was bought by F. B. Crittall, from whose workshop the Crittall Manufacturing Company sprang. Continuing along Bank Street we pass some of the best shops for the 1851 shopper: Buddens, the linen draper; Claydons, the grocer; James Nash, fishmonger and fruiterer; and John Smith, gun maker and china dealer. The street remained narrow right up to the White Hart, for today's wide space is the result of a war-time bomb which destroyed the street frontage. A tour like this could go on much longer, but we are now back at our starting point and the White Hart is just opening its doors, so I think it is time to try a little more 'Brayntry Beer'.

No. 1. TILL. **ESSEX BANK.**

No. 5775 BRAINTREE, 3 June 1886.

Received of Mr Jno Eley's Exors

the Sum of One hundred & fifteen Pounds, 9/4

For SPARROW, TUFNELL & Co.

£115. 9. 4 C. H. Packer

J. H. Goodchild's Exorship

BRAINTREE Bank. No 45 Aug 16th 1895

Messrs Sparrow, Tufnell & Co.

Pay Miss E. Goodchild OR ORDER

Fifty pounds

£50—0—0 M. S. Goodchild, Saml Goodchild } Exors

This Draft must be signed at the back by the Party to whom it is made payable.

LONDON AGENTS, BARCLAY, BEVAN & Co.

ONE PENNY

No 26 Augt. 1897

BARCLAY & COMPANY, LIMITED.

BANKERS

With which has been incorporated

Messrs Sparrow, Tufnell & Co.

BRAINTREE.

Pay Messrs Pyke & Son — or Order

Two pounds 10/5 —

£2. 10. 5 M. S. Goodchild, Saml Goodchild } Exors of G. H. Goodchild deceased

HEAD OFFICE, 54 LOMBARD STREET, LONDON, E.C. This Draft must be signed at the back by the Party to whom it is made payable.

ESSEX BANK

ONE PENNY

OPPOSITE ABOVE: A till receipt for Sparrow, Tufnell & Co. 1886. CENTRE: Sparrow, Tufnell & Co cheque, 1895, and BELOW: Barclay & Co cheque, 1897. LEFT: Barclays Bank, formerly Sparrow, Tufnell & Co. RIGHT: Frederick Smoothy, solicitor, of Rayne Road. (ERO/JA) BELOW: High Street and the King's Head, c1840. (ERO/JA)

LEFT: The George Inn, New Street. (ERO/JA) RIGHT: Joscelyne's, New Street after restoration, and BELOW: before restoration. The George Inn's lantern bracket can still be seen. (DAB)

ABOVE: Bank Street c1920. The shops on the left—first Blomfields, then Parmenter's ladies outfitters—were destroyed by a Second World War bomb on 14 February, 1941. The central 'island' divides Swan Street from Bank Street. (NG) LEFT: Swan Street, c1920. (NG) RIGHT: Pasfield's Boot & Shoe shop, Bank Street, opposite Woolworths, c1900. (NG)

SPECIAL

SHOW OF SPRING GOODS

NOW ON VIEW.

Wall Papers, choice designs, from 1½d. roll.

Paints, ready mixed, all colours, 3lbs. 1s., 2s. 3d. 7lbs.

Carpets, Rugs, Linoleums, Mats, Mattings, and Floor Coverings at special low prices.

Brooms, Brushes, Floor Polishers, Stains, Varnishes, and all Requisites for Spring Cleaning

Mangles, Washing and Wringing Machines.

Garden Rollers, Arches, and Garden Tools of every description.

Wood Expanding Trellis, Wire Nettings.

Durexo Washable Distemper, all colours.

Special Show of Perambulators and Mail Carts in new designs.

Several Second-Hand Mail Carts For Sale Cheap.

J. H. MOODY,

COMPLETE
HOUSE FURNISHER,

RAILWAY-STREET, BRAINTREE.

ABOVE: Swan Inn, Bank Street, 1981. LEFT: Swan Inn from Little Square. The date on the beam is 1590. RIGHT: Advertisement in *The Essex Newsman*, 1907.

ABOVE: J.H. Moody, 'Universal Provider', Railway Street, (NG)
BELOW: Osborn's leather shop, Little Square. (NG)

IT CARRIES WEIGHT.

Weight is the all-important property of a garden roller, and the weight of the Ironcrete Roller, compared with its size, is remarkable. Furthermore its low price places it within the reach of all home gardeners.

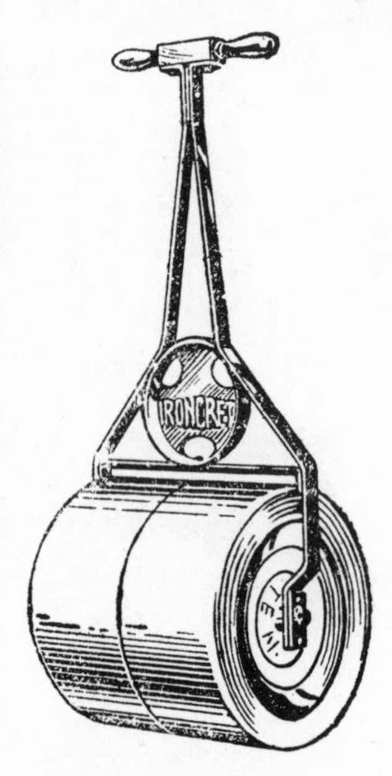

Ironcrete Rollers

are better than ever this year.

The cylinder is made in two parts with rounded edges for easy turning, the patent bearings make running easy, and the handle is fitted with a special support, keeping it off the turf.

It is a perfect roller for lawns, paths, etc., and made to last a lifetime.

196 lbs.	14 inch	...	**28/6.**
224 lbs.	16 inch	...	**32/6.**
336 lbs.	18 inch	...	**45/-.**

Advertisement for Crittall and Winterton, ironmongers in *Halstead & Colne Valley Gazette,* 1929.

VIEWS OF THE SHOWROOMS

FOR

Dining Room, .
Drawing Room,
Bedroom . . .
Furniture and .
Appointments .

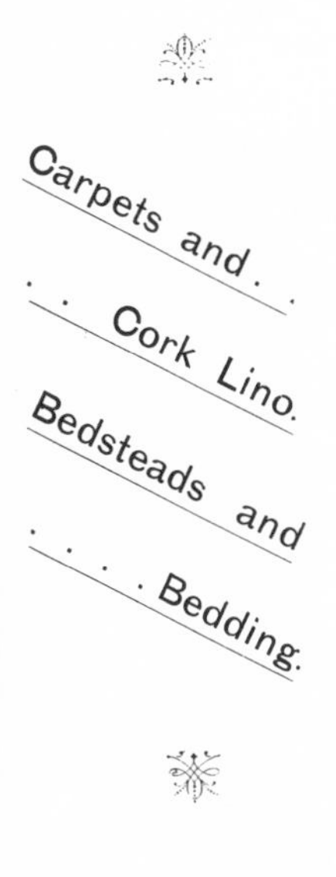

AT

HENRY JOSCELYNE'S, BRAINTREE.

Nowhere is the modern artistic feeling better shown than in the prevailing style of . . .

Furniture for the Dining Room.

THIS DEPARTMENT IS FULL OF INTEREST AT JOSCELYNE'S.

We START with

Dining Room Suites, . . .

In Leather Cloth, well built and finished, at . . . .

£4 10 0.

Saddlebag Suites . .

we offer at

£5 15 0

And those in

Figured Velvet

£6 15 0

Typical Modern Dining Room Furniture.
The above Suite in Pegamoid or Utrecht Velvet - - - - - **£10 10 0.**

Artistic Modern

Dining Room Suites . . .

In Solid Walnut and Fumed Oak, in all the best coverings. Ranging in price from

£8 15 0 upwards.

In stock in great variety.

Kerbs,

In Black, Copper, and Brass,

Fire . . Implements.

Coal Boxes.

QUAINT OAK SIDEBOARDS AND SUITES TO MATCH. . . .

JOSCELYNE'S STOCK . . .

Represents the present taste in Artistic and Economical Furnishing.

3

Catalogue for Henry Joscelyne's shop.

Our Special Features in Bedroom Furniture are soundness of construction and artistic design.

These are secured in our solid suites produced by machinery of the latest type.

Solid, Substantial Satin Walnut . .

Bedroom Suite,

Wardrobe, Dressing Chest, Washstand, each 3 ft. wide - - -

£7 15 0.

Dressing Chest and Washstand

In Satin Walnut,

£3 18 6.

Large Satin Walnut

Chest of Drawers, Wash Stand, Dressing Table,

Modern, Smart, and Well made.

£4 19 6.

LAWSON, PHOTO, BRAINTREE.

Joscelyne's Historic Showroom for Bedroom Suites.
Suites in stock from 5 to 25 guineas.

REMOVING.

HOW IT USED TO BE DONE!

THE LAST PAGE,

And we have not even mentioned a great part of our large and varied Stock.

We have Twenty Show and Stock Rooms and they are all full to the door.

The secret of our increasing trade is that we buy and sell for . . . **CASH** (and by saving bad debts, and turning the money over quickly, we can give customers such **immense advantages.**

FREE DELIVERY WITHIN 100 MILES.

HOW WE DO IT NOW.
Let us give you an Estimate.

We are just the people to furnish a Working Man's Home . . . .

A 3-roomed Cottage costs **£7 7 0**
To Furnish from us.

A 4-roomed House we fit up for **£13 10 0**

Stop beating your old Carpets.

Don't pay Fancy Price for Pianos

We can sell you a fine instrument, with all the latest improvements, perfectly new, for **15 Guineas.**

A really Tip-Top Piano

With beautiful marqueterie front and rich round tone, well made and finished, for . . . . **20 Guineas.**

These two instruments are often priced at 24 & 30 guineas by Hire Purchase Dealers.

SECOND-HAND PIANOS VERY CHEAP.

WE HAVE A FINE RANGE OF

Framed Engravings, Photogravures, and Oil Paintings

PALM AND FERN STANDS.

The "Gritzner" Family Sewing Machine

At **£2 12 6** and **£3 3 0** is a marvellous machine, at a marvellously low price. Call and test it.

Let us send you a few New Ones on Approval.

Henry Joscelyne's catalogue.

The New Age

In 1898 a latter-day Garden of Eden was discovered just past Chelmsford. Here, according to one traveller it was possible to 'rejoice in the guileless rusticity of the peasant-populated region'. But the same traveller, once 'within the walls of Braintree', saw a dramatic change. He was now surrounded by 'large ironworks and the swarthy, sinewy, and grimy sons of Tubal Cain'.

What then had happened to the quiet market we saw in 1851? Even allowing for our traveller's exaggeration, the character of the town was certainly changing. The reason for this was clear—the depression in Essex farming which lasted throughout the last quarter of the century. As our commentator of 1898 put it, 'the agricultural depression which had menaced the prosperity of the town had awakened her citizens to commercial enterprise, and made of Braintree a manufacturing centre'.

The new factory-based industry sprang, suitably enough, from one of the many small workshop businesses spawned by the market. The ironmongers and agricultural machine makers outgrew their jobbing work and laid the foundation of the 20th century engineering industry. The Crittall Manufacturing Company started from Francis Crittall's ironmonger's shop in Bank Street; Lake & Elliot Ltd was created when W. B. Lake, who ran a bicycle shop in New Street, was joined by E. F. Elliot in 1896; and Joseph Bradbury & Sons Ltd took root when young Joseph, the son of Walters' Silk Mill engineer, began as a tool-maker in what were more recently Brentex's premises in New Street.

By the time Crittalls became a limited concern in 1889, they had already been doing well for several years, particularly after the destruction caused by the Colchester earthquake which caused much rebuilding. The company built the Manor Works in 1893 and developed the production of steel windows—one of the products of the Bank Street workshop. As the firm grew, they built other factories in nearby towns. The most remarkable of these was the creation of a new industrial village at Silver End. This was begun in 1926 when the company built a factory on 200 acres of farmland they had acquired. The new village—complete with modern drainage, electric light, communal laundry, cinema, workers' club, restaurant, sports and play areas— was almost space-age in its modernity by contrast with rural Essex. Today, the distinctive flat-rooved houses still dominate the village, while similar 'Crittall houses' also stand in Braintree at Cressing Road.

The new partnership of Lake and Elliot moved to the Albion Works in Rayne Road in 1896. Here they made 'cycle tools and vehicle jacks. Ten years later, the expanding company moved to the New Albion Works on Chapel Hill. There they installed a steel foundry and what was reputedly the first 'electric arc furnace' in Britain. Before long the firm was large enough to advertise in *Jane's Fighting Ships* of 1914 and to be one of the first Essex factories to build a motor car.

Braintree's former serenity was now broken by the 'roar and shriek of factory horns' and invited comparison with the Midlands towns of Wolverhampton and Dudley. One observer predicted: 'in the future, more or less distant, the drowsy passenger travelling on the railway at midnight through Braintree, will watch with curiosity the many radiating glares hovering over the numerous ironworks around, whose fiery furnaces are not permitted to exhaust themselves'. Yet we get a very different picture of the town from a young lady reporter who visited the town in 1902. She had been sent by her editor to 'the quiet Essex village of Braintree' to find the factory where the Coronation mantle was being woven. 'This is the way to Warner's factory', a rosy-cheeked girl is reported to have told her and she 'could not but compare the good appearance of these girls with the factory "hands" one sees thronging the cotton mills in the North, with shawls tied over their heads'.

Which of these contradictory views of the town are we to trust? The truth is that they were describing two industries—one old and one new—which existed side by side in the town. But it was engineering which brought growth. At the start of the 20th century the combined population of Braintree and Bocking was 8,677. This was just 37 more than in 1881. Yet, by the outbreak of war in 1914, the total had topped 10,000 as more jobs were created in engineering. No longer was Braintree a town of weavers, workshop craftsmen, and tradesmen.

Life in Edwardian Braintree accelerated away from the 19th century pattern. By 1900 the franchise had been extended and some attention, at least, was being turned upon the gulf between rich and poor. Like other towns Braintree was providing a wider range of social services and, of course, health, poverty, and educational matters were by now under centralised control. The quality of life for most was improving. The town itself took on a smarter appearance and more public buildings were going up. In 1888, the Public Gardens, given by Sydney and Sarah Courtauld, were opened. The celebrations rivalled those of Victoria's Jubilee the year before. The town band were there—known as the 'Braintree Resters' because they paused for a drink between each item. A torch-light procession, led by the town's Fire Brigade, paraded through the streets, and a huge bonfire was lit in the fields at the corner of Coggeshall Road and Courtauld Road. The menu for the celebration dinner listed: Roast and Boiled Fowls, Roast Ducks, Roast Beef and Mutton, Pressed Beef, Ham, Pigeon, and Rabbit Pies. These were washed down with Champagne at 7s a bottle or Bass's beer at 6d.

The Braintree High School was another beneficiary of the Courtaulds. The land was given by Mrs Sydney Courtauld of Bocking Place, and the opening was performed by her son, William Julian Courtauld, in 1907. W. J. Courtauld did more than anyone to supply Braintree with public buildings. He gave the hospital which bears his name, a recreation ground, financed the Town Hall which opened in 1928, and donated the fountain and Nurses' Home which stand next to St Michael's.

For the first time there was a wide choice of entertainment available to the working man and his family. Two marching bands played at fetes, school treats, church parades, and in the Public Gardens on Sunday evenings. The Town Band was entirely brass, while the Excelsior combined brass with reeds. A little higher on the cultural scale, Braintree could boast three orchestras. The Braintree Musical Society gave concerts in the Institute, the 'Pleasant Sunday Afternoon Orchestra' performed in London Road Chapel, while the Lawson family 'orchestra' played mostly at private engagements.

The Braintree Gordons Football Club played on the Fairfield and their reputation spread throughout Essex. They once reached the final of the Essex Senior Cup, but they folded about 1898. Their place was taken by a team from the Manor Works—the forerunners of the present Braintree & Crittal Athletic—who also played on the Fairfield until someone in authority decided to build the Town Hall in the middle of their pitch. There was a cycling club, and a gymnastics team which met at the Institute. Around 1898 a swimming club was formed, taking their name—the Blackwater Swimming Club—from the river they used near Straits Mill, Bocking. In 1913 the club moved to the new Rose Hill Baths. During the period at Bocking, several popular galas and regular Christmas morning races were held. Another feature of the river was pleasure steamer trips between Strait's and Cane's Mills. The fare was 6d.

Yet there was still poverty, and what gave an edge to it were the vast inequalities of wealth. When Major Sebag Montefiore sold Stisted Hall in 1915, the estate included farms, cottages, and public houses extending throughout the village and into neighbouring parishes. In all the 'squire' of Stisted Hall—the 18th century title seems appropriate—owned 3,395 acres. The rent roll was worth over £4,000 at a time when the yearly wage of farm labourers was around £60. The Hall was a Georgian-style mansion with 18 principal bed and dressing rooms, 5 bathrooms, 'ample accommodation for servants', stabling for 14 horses and 3 motor-cars, 128 acres of parkland, and 170 acres of woodland for hunting and shooting.

But the stirrings of change were being felt. The First World War accelerated change. In May 1918 the Maldon Constituency Labour Party was formed. *The Braintree & Witham Times* reported: 'On Saturday afternoon a meeting of Labour representatives convened by the Braintree Trades Council was held at the White Hart, Witham to consider the question of a Labour Candidate for the Maldon Constituency'. In the General Election later that year, the Labour Party came within 2,000 votes of winning. The Conservative candidate, Sir Fortescue Flannery was returned to Westminster, while the Liberals, in decline, came a poor third. After the short post-war boom, the country had its first taste of the economic depression which lasted for nearly two decades. The 1923 election heralded the first Labour Government, led by Ramsay Macdonald. It was a momentous year locally too. Just five years after its inaugural meeting, the Maldon Constituency Labour Party had its first Member of Parliament—Valentine Crittall, the local industrialist.

When the Labour Government fell in 1924 the result was reflected locally and Crittall was soundly defeated. The years until the second outbreak of war saw unemployment soar. The Means Test became the bane of the swelling numbers of unemployed. A *Braintree & Witham Times* headline tells the story: '2,000 UNEMPLOYED AT BRAINTREE WORKHOUSE'. The editorial, titled 'Means Test Tragedies', reflects the growing concern in the town in 1932: 'The unemployment problem in the Braintree and Witham areas becomes more acute every day. It is reaching alarming proportions, and much misery and distress is now emerging...Almost daily in Braintree the unemployed hold meetings. There were great gatherings at the Clock House and at the fountain in the Market Place. At the latter, fully 800 people were present. Protest was raised against the Means Test and the reductions in the allowances to the unemployed'. The scars of these years were a long time healing.

Yet, despite these upheavals, the town grew at a faster rate than at any time during the previous century. By 1939 the population of the Braintree Urban District was over 15,000. The town no longer consisted of two parishes, for in 1934 they had been amalgamated into a single Urban District. The age of the council house had arrived. Braintree UDC had built 735, mostly in Coggeshall Road-Cressing Road and Panfield Lane areas, by the time war broke out. Brick tentacles were groping deeper into the fields which surrounded the town. Along Cressing Road, London Road, and towards Bocking, a thin ribbon of brick and concrete was crossing the river valleys which had been the town's natural boundaries. The age of the semi-detached, the private car, and the wireless were reaching Braintree.

Then suddenly the lights went out. Unlike the earlier war, 1939-45 was a civilian war. Every town in Britain was made frighteningly aware that the battle was being fought not only in distant lands but also above their heads. Essex was hit very badly because of its position on the airlanes to London. Many bombs left over from the 'Blitz' on London were dropped on Braintree as a last hostile gesture before the German bombers droned back across the North Sea.

In February 1941 the town suffered a direct hit. At 9 pm, just as the crowd was pouring out of the Embassy Cinema, there was a flash of brilliant light in the sky over Bank Street. The entire town shook, windows were broken and, as far away as Fairfield Road, the Post Office doors were blasted open. The bomb had fallen on the corner of Bank Street and Coggeshall Road. Amazingly the White Hart Inn was left standing, but the opposite corner was completely destroyed.

Three people were killed by the bomb, one of them a young boy hit by flying glass as he looked out of a nearby window. The blackened, charred site was a chilling reminder of death to all Braintree people. Worse was to come, though, as the Germans launched the V1 flying bomb (or Doodlebug) attacks on London and the South-East. These bombs played cruelly on the nerves as you listened to the throb of their engines, praying they would not cut out.One of the first to be unleashed fell on Braintree. The Home Guard (Post Office Signals Company) were fire-watching on top of the Fairfield Road Post Office when the flying bomb passed over the town, cut out, and fell in Notley Road close to Notley Place. So powerful was the blast that it nearly knocked the watchers off their platform atop the Post Office. The Signals Company drew on men from the Post Offices at Braintree, Halstead, and Sudbury. But Braintree also had its own Home Guard battalion, numbering about 200, who met at the Drill Hall in Victoria Road. They were ready as a last line of defence if needed though there were times, as when the Signals accidentally blasted a hole in Hicks' 'bus garage in Fairfield Road, when it seemed their preparations placed the local inhabitants in more danger than the Germans.

As the war proceeded, more and more people were involved, including women and children. Women joined the armed services, and around Braintree they worked as 'land girls' or as munitions workers at Crittalls and the town's engineering works. The austerity of war-time meant an emphasis on 'fair shares for all' and a more equal society in terms of both class and sex. When peace finally returned, expectations of employment and the quality of life were very different from before. Braintree moved, like other towns and villages in Britain, into a different, modern world. Yet, the town's long history continued to shape its growth and the way of life of its people.

Ornamental water, Public Gardens—gift of the Courtaulds, opened in 1888. (NG)

. BRAINTREE & BOCKING .

PUBLIC GARDENS.

Rules & Regulations.

1. The Gardens will be open to the Public every day in the year, from 8 o'clock a.m. until half an hour after sunset.

2. All Persons excepting Tramps, Beggars, and disorderly or intoxicated persons will be admitted free to the Gardens.

3. Children under 10 years of age will not be admitted to the Inner Garden unless accompanied by a grown person.

4. No Perambulators will be allowed in the Inner Garden after 2 o'clock p.m.

5. No Dogs will be allowed in the Gardens.

6. No Picnic Parties will be allowed in the Gardens and no intoxicating liquors shall be brought in.

7. Persons not sober or using bad language or behaving in a disorderly manner, or in any way annoying other Visitors, will be expelled and liable to be prosecuted.

8. Persons committing any nuisance or doing any kind of damage, or wilfully infringing the Rules will be expelled and liable to be prosecuted.

9. Football, Cricket and other Games will not be allowed so as to cause inconvenience or damage to the Visitors.

10. The Garden Keeper has strict orders to stop stone throwing, unnecessary noise or rough behaviour, and to keep order throughout the Gardens.

The Trustees earnestly request Visitors to assist the Garden Keeper in carrying out the above Regulations which are made solely in the interest of those using the Gardens.

By order of the Trustees,

E. HOLMES, CLERK.

November 26th, 1888.

FOOTBALL.

Halstead Charity Cup.

LAKE AND ELLIOT'S v. 1st SUFFOLK REGIMENT.

At Braintree. About 250 spectators watched a very ragged display. Allen cried off at the last minute, Mann going inside-right and Firmin left-half, otherwise Lakes were well represented. For the first 20 minutes Lakes had all the play but could not score, Harris in goal playing a superb game. Jones missed by inches. G. Osborne scored for Lakes, only for Billington to soon equalise for the Soldiers. The game continued scrappy, half-time arriving with the score of one goal each. For the first 10 minutes in the second half the Soldiers had the best of the game and Hales gave them the lead. From this point Lakes took up the play and Bell equalised. From the restart Lakes scored again, through Jones, and he also gave Lakes the lead, and just after he scored two more goals in quick succession. The Soldiers could not stay the pace and C. Mann added another, to be followed by one from Jones. Lakes ran out winners by 7 goals to 2.

THE GAMES OF LAWN TENNIS AND BOWLS.

NOTICE.

THE GAME OF LAWN TENNIS.

The charge for a Tennis Court is 6d. for each hour irrespective of the number of players. This charge must be paid in advance to the Garden-keeper.

Upon applying at the Lodge, the Courts may be engaged after 2 p.m., three days in advance, but no person can engage a Court in advance for more than an hour.

The Charge to be paid when the Court is engaged.

Players must provide their own Rackets and Balls.

THE GAME OF BOWLS.

The Charge for playing is ½d. per head for each half-hour. This charge must be paid in advance to the Garden-keeper.

Upon applying at the Lodge the Bowls may be engaged after 2 p.m., three days in advance but no person can engage them in advance for more than half-an-hour on the same day, except for match playing, and then for not more than one hour on the same day.

The Charge to be paid when the engagement is made.

By Order,

Edw. HOLMES,

Clerk to the Trustees.

COUNTY HIGH SCHOOL,

BRAINTREE.

HEAD MASTER: F. J. WEAVER, M.A. (London).

THIS SCHOOL, for BOYS and GIRLS of 12 years of age and upwards, will be OPENED at the beginning of MAY, 1907. Applications for Admission are invited. Fee, Two Guineas per Term. The Head Master is now resident at Braintree, and will be pleased to meet Parents or Guardians by appointment. Prospectus and Registration Form may be obtained from the Clerk to the School Governors.

N.B.—The ENTRANCE EXAMINATION will be held on Tuesday, 16th April, 1907, and the Term will commence on Thursday, 2nd May. Notice will be given to registered students.

J. GLEAVE,
Hollywood,
Braintree.

OPPOSITE LEFT: Rules and Regulations, Public Gardens, 1888. ABOVE: Fountain, a gift of William Julian Courtauld. BELOW: Football report from the *Halstead & Colne Valley Gazette,* 1929. ABOVE: Tennis and bowls notices, Public Gardens, 1888. LEFT: County High School before the official opening, 27 April 1907, (DW) and RIGHT: Advertisement for pupils in *The Essex Newsman,* 1907.

ABOVE: Laying the foundation stone of the Town Hall. (ERO/JA) LEFT: Council Chamber, 1928. (ERO/JA) RIGHT: The old Town Hall after the Council moved to Causeway House, 1981. BELOW: Official opening of Rose Hill Baths, 1914. (ERO/JA)

LEFT: Sun Lido, Rayne Road. (ERO/JA) RIGHT: Camera Club caught on the other side of the lens. (DW) BELOW: Church Street, Bocking c1910. (NG)

Rover

"I offer you beauty of line and finish; a genuine Weymann body with folding roof, soft leather upholstery, with front seats separately and independently adjustable; comfortable room for 4 passengers: ample accommodation for your luggage in the trunk that sits so snugly on my tail. You can have me in brown, black, blue or red; I have wire wheels, and you may choose them in cream, black, red or green. I am equipped with all the fittings you desire. I offer you the world's supreme value." Thus speaks the Rover Sportsman's Coupe.

This is the smartest light car
—and with a TWO Years' Guarantee—

SPORTSMAN'S COUPE
£269
SALOON - - £250

—the Rover Sportsman's Coupe

Frank A. Bloomfield,

BRAINTREE 'Phone 5. **HALSTEAD** Phone 12.

OPPOSITE LEFT: Advertisement in the *Halstead & Colne Valley Gazette,* 1929. RIGHT: Embassy Cinema, 1981. BELOW: Picture Palace, Fairfield Road. (NG) ABOVE: Braintree 1st Scouts Troop. (NG) BELOW: Braintree Scouts at camp (NG)

ABOVE: Braintree Salvationists Singing Company, 1927. (NG) CENTRE: Warner's carnival group. Braintree's 750th anniversary, 1949. (WA) BELOW: Coronation procession, June 1953. (NG)

Postscript

Almost 2,000 years have passed since the Roman army, pursuing Boadicea, created the Braintree crossroads on the ancient Stane Street. Today the town which grew up there houses 30,000 people and gives its name to a parliamentary constituency. Cunnington, the town's historian in the 19th century, would probably have wished to mark the latter fact by a new history, as he did after the 1832 Reform Act gave Braintree new parliamentary status. But Cunnington would be confused by the town today. Twice this century its status has changed. In 1934, the separate units of Braintree and Bocking merged to form a single Urban District. More recently, in 1974, the town became the administrative centre of the Braintree District, which has a population of well over 100,000.

Most of all Cunnington would be struck by the town's surge of growth, as if it had just passed through adolescence. Its limbs, those long arms of ribbon housing development, filled out with the bulging muscles of residential and industrial estates, have grown rapidly. The Braintree voice has altered; the accents of London speech are heard as often as the no-longer-so-broad Essex sounds. The complexion has changed too, with the last few decades sweeping away much that had survived for hundreds of years.

The looming presence of London is now keenly felt; in the 1960s the former Urban District Council combined with the Greater London Council to provide 1,200 homes for London families. Large numbers of Braintree people commute to work in the Capital, and 1977 introduced a direct electrified rail link with London. Other transport changes, most notably the proposed expansion of Stansted airport, are likely to affect the town. And, at the time of writing, the town's most famous firm—Courtaulds—has announced the closure of its Braintree Mill, 171 years after George Courtauld set up his business at a water-mill on Chapel Hill.

Yet the marks of old age remain: the narrow streets and alleyways of the mediaeval town, the clothiers' houses in Bradford Street, the weather-boarded silk mill in South Street. Sadly, modern surgery has removed some familiar features. The Corn Exchange, with its sturdy, bold clock, no longer surveys the High Street and the cattle-market is buried under a supermarket of brobdignagian proportions. Yet, sad though this is, it shows that Braintree still has the vigour and adaptability which has characterised its long history.

LEFT: Braintree College of Further Education. RIGHT: Courtauld's Braintree Mill, 1981. CENTRE: Courtauld's 'Old Factory', which has housed the silk firms of Walters and Warners, and the engineering firm, Bradbury's. BELOW: Causeway House, the new home of Braintree District Council, 1981.

Index

Bibliography

General Sources

William Addison, *Essex Heyday* (1949).
D. H. Allen (ed.), *Essex Quarter Sessions Order Book, 1652-1661.*
John Booker, *Essex and the Industrial Revolution* (1974).
A. F. J. Brown, *Essex at Work 1700-1815* (1969).
A. C. Edwards, *A History of Essex* (1978).
F. G. Emmison, *Early Essex Town Meetings* (1970).
F. G. Emmison, *Elizabethan Life: Essex Gentry's Wills*
F. G. Emmison, *Elizabethan Life: Home, Work, & Land* (1976).
Essex Archaeology & History.
Essex Directories: *Kelly's, Pigot's,* & *White's.* (Various Years).
Industries of the Eastern Counties, Pub by the British Industrial Publishing Company (1890).
Philip Morant, *The History & Antiquities of the County of Essex* (1768).
Muilman, *History of Essex* 2 vols (1772).
R. Newcourt, *Repertorium Ecclesiasticum* (1710).
Norden, *Description of Essex* (1594) (Camden Society Reprint).
N. Pevsner, *The Buildings of England: Essex* (2nd Edition 1965).
P. H. Reaney, *The Place Names of Essex* (1935).
Victoria County History of Essex 5 vols (London & Oxford, 1903-56).
A. Young, *General View of the Agriculture of the County of Essex* (1813).

Local and Primary Sources

Winifred Ashwell, *Essex & the 'Lyon'* (1971).
Winifred Ashwell, *The Company of the Four & Twenty* (1970).
Michael Baker, *The Poor in Georgian & Victorian Braintree* (1976).
Malcolm J. Baker, *The Revolt of the Field in North Essex 1840-75* (1979).
Braintree & Bocking Official Guide Pub Burrow & Co. (4th Edition).
H. Bury, *New Mills, Braintree* in *Essex Countryside* (June 1979).
D. C. Coleman, *Courtaulds. An Economic & Social History* 2 vols. (1969).
J. Corley, *Braintree's Silk Remnants* in *Essex Countryside* (1979).
J. Cunnington, *A History of the Ancient Town of Braintree* MSS 2 vols (1833) Deposited at ERO (Acc No 5052)
J. Cunnington, *Architectural & Church Notes in the County of Essex 1790-99* MS Deposited at ERO (T/P 80).
M. Cunnington & S. Warner, *Braintree & Bocking* (1906)
Friends of Bradford Street, *Discovering Bradford Street* (1978)
A. Hills, *Braintree Market Print, 1826; Braintree Doctors in Olden Days; Old 'New Street';* and other articles and miscellaneous papers deposited at the ERO (T/Z 20)
F. Hobson, Miscellaneous papers, off-prints, & correspondence belonging to this former Editor of the *Braintree & Witham Times* (1930-39), deposited at the ERO (T/P 116 1-47)
Ann Hoffmann, *Bocking Deanery, The Story of an Essex Peculiar* (1976)
Alec Hunter, A History of Warner & Sons Ltd. Reprinted from the *Journal of the Textile Institute* Vol 41, No 2 (Feb 1950)
Rev J. W. Kenworthy, A Relic Found at Braintree in *Essex Review* XX, pp 87-90 (1911)
Rev J. W. Kenworthy, Historic Braintree in *Essex Review* XX, pp 34-41 (1911).
Maldon Constituency Labour Party: The First Fifty Years (1968).
Myth, Braintree: Its Commercial Importance (1898)
Myth, Historic Braintree: Its Mysteries & Tragedy (1899)
W. F. Quin, *Bocking Independent Meeting House 1707-1957* (Anniversary booklet).
J. Rayner, *An Account of the Textile Industry in Bocking,* unpublished typescript written c1950-55, deposited at the ERO (T/Z 27)
Savill Family Papers & Notebook, 1754-1827. Deposited at the ERO (D/DCd)
I. A. Scotchman, From Axe to A.C. in *The Railway Magazine* (Oct 1977)
B. S. Wood, *Braintree & West Essex Co-operative Society Ltd. 1864-1914* (1914).

Census Returns, Maps, and Newspapers

Census of 1831 (ERO D/DU 65/83 and Q/CR 2/8/1)
Census of 1851 (ERO T/A 208/5)
Chapman & André Map of Essex (1777)
Map and Survey, 1814 by J. H. Clayton (ERO D/DU 65/78)
Tithe Award Map and Survey (ERO D/P 264/ 27/1, /2)
O.S. Maps, Braintree and Bocking (1805; 1874-5; 1919 (Rev 1939); 1955; 1973)
Braintree & Bocking Advertiser
Braintree & Witham Times
Essex Chronicle
Essex County Standard.

Subscribers

Presentation Copies

1 Braintree and Bocking District Council
2 Essex County Council
3 Braintree Public Library
4 Braintree Heritage Centre
5 Essex County Record Office
6 Braintree Museum
7 Councillor Malcolm Bryan
8 John Corley

9 Michael Baker
10 Clive & Carolyn Birch
11 Mrs B.M. Harding
12 T.A. Knott
13 Miss J.G. Cartridge
14 P.J. Gordon
15 Mrs Margaret A. Stratford
16 J.W. White
17 Mrs S.M. Birmingham
18 R.F. Cornell
19 Mrs B.D. Martin
20 A.D. Smith
21 A.J. Fletcher
22 Mrs Goodwin
23 Adrian Mott
24 Mrs H. Drury
25 Guy Eagling
26 T. Brunning
27 H.W. Gowers
28 Mrs Y. Morton
29 R.F. Gentry
30 Mrs R. Daniels
31 Mrs J. Wakefield
32 J.S. Finch
33 Mrs M. Adlington
34 Mrs P. Ratcliff
35 Mrs M.J. Wood
36 Peter Chard
37 David Read
38 Malcolm Read
39 Victoria & Albert Museum
40 Leicester Library
41 B.S. Kiek
42 Mrs B. Humphries
43 Jane Harrington
44 Mrs G.R. Dixon
45 Mrs S.L. Wood
46 J.A.J. Farmer
47 Mrs A.E. Wren
48 B.J. Hockridge
49 Mrs V.J. Bick
50 Mrs B. Brown
51 D. Lacey
52 Mrs K.G. West
53 C.L. Parker
54 Mrs W.B. Usher
55 Mrs B.M. Jones
56 Mrs E.A. Felton
57 E.J. Ager
58 L.C. Pinner
59 P.R. Brown
60 Mrs Sandra A. Clarke
61 Mrs S. Glover
62 Mrs S. Thaker
63 Mrs S.A. Boyce
64 Mrs L. Bibbey
65 R.W. Beaumont
66 Mrs D.J. Lawrence
67 Mrs S. Welham
68 G.R. Townsend
69 Miss S. Younger
70 Mrs K.P. Meldram
71 Miss R.E. Pepper
72 Mrs P.A. Penny
73 Mrs J. Keable
74 L.K. Feltham
75 D.J. Matthams
76 R.E. Frost
77 John Wright
78 M.W. Young
79 A.S. Butcher
80 Mrs J. Skingsley
81 G.R. Cornell
82 H.R. Cook
83 Mrs J.F. Swetenham
84 T.E. Byford
85 Mrs D.M. Hutley
86 Mrs B.M. Kibble
87 P.J. Smith
88 L. Bolden
89 Mrs J.A. Mold
90 Mrs B.E.E. Godfrey
91 Miss J.M. Wilson
92 Mrs J.A. Davies
93 Mr & Mrs R.B. Thomas
94 R.C. Cook
95 J.A. Cook
96 Mrs M. French
97 Mrs O.E. Brittain
98 C.J. Townrow
99 L.G. Gage
100, 101 B. Barker
102 Nicki Gowers
103 P.F. Ware
104 T.D. Robertson JP
105 Mrs P. Cannon
106 T. Relf
107 Mrs Jean Gellatly
108 C.R. Hetherington
109 T.D. Jones
110 R. Oliver
111 Mrs D.P. Goodchild
112 Mrs J.P. Suckling
113 Mrs M.T. Dyer
114 Mrs M. Youngman
115 Mrs White
116 I.D.M. Baird
117 Mrs P.J. Garner
118 David Jarman
119 Mrs M. Crisp
120 Alan Hodge
121, 122 Mrs Margaret Hammond
123 Mrs R. Cook
124 Mrs C.A. Phair
125 Mrs C. Pinney
126 Mrs Sugden
127 Mrs S.D. Goodey
128 A.G. Potter
129 D.J. Boreham
130 Mrs Everard
131 Mrs A.L. Pryke
132 Mrs P. Davis
133 Mrs Muriel Dixon
134 Mrs C. Camfield
135 E.J. Stiff
136 M.P. Aguallo
137 Christine Wakeling
138 Martin L. Perry
139 John Joyce
140 G.T. Burton
141 A.G. Foster
142 K. Goff
143 Mrs J.M. Tokley
144 Mrs O.G. Cutts
145 R. Humphries
146 Cyril E.G. Warner
147 G.G. Brock
148 Mrs R. Goodwin
149 A. Parish
150 Mrs P. Prackford
151 Mr Thorogood
152 Mrs P.M. Cremer
153 Derek Bircher
154 Mrs Sylvia Challis
155 Miss P.E. Vincent
156 J. Clements
157 Norman Holmes
158 Mollie Webster
159 Colin Davis
160 Mrs A.E. Turnbull
161 H.H. Agate
162 Mrs S.A. Hayes
163 J.E. Kearley
164 Mrs M. Jones
165 Mrs Jean Lambert
166 C. McIlroy
167 G. Sturman
168 Pauline J. Smith
169 A. Harrow
170 B. Russell
171 C.H. Osborne
172 P.R. Smith
173 A.E.J. Fletcher
174 Miss L. Prior
175 E.W. Peagram
176 Mrs M. Gardner
177 R.J. Galley
178 A. Thurgood
179 Mrs J.A. Bishop
180 Mrs E. Loring
181 Mrs A.C. Ratcliffe
182 Mr & Mrs E.A. Peachey
183 Miss Susan Angel
184, 185 Mrs Reed
186 P. Haygreen
187 Terry Peter Surrey

188 R.E. Barton
189 T.J. Rowland
190 Mrs M.R. Williams
191 Mrs E. Clark
192 Mrs E.T. Gormley
193 J.N. Cross
194 Richard Allen
195 F. Rogers
196 Mrs D. Lodge
197 Heather A. Alvanez
198 M. Moss
199 A. Austin
200 Jennifer Catlin
201 S.L. Sutton
202 F.E. Card
203 Mrs E.R. Ridley
204 C.S. Smith
205 C.W. Frame
206 Alan Reeder
207 Eric Gole
208 Hazel Doyle
209 Donald John Moore
210 William David Whitehurst
211 Mrs K. Cordell
212 Mrs V.M. Fitch
213 Wg Cdr E.J. Dickie
214 J.L. Lindsay
215 Mrs M. Haskell
216 Mrs M. Pudney
217 W.S. Butcher
218 A.F. Whybrow
219 C.A. Cole
220 K.L. Dodman
221 Mrs J. Grace
222 Mrs Larner
223 Miss M.G. Allen
224 Miss D.M. Johnson
225 V.M. Marsh
226 Mrs R. Williams
227 J. Williams
228 D. Welham
229 D.P. Bearman
230 Mrs L. Bewley
231 Mrs J. Groom
232 N.P. Lewin
233 Norma Morrison
234 Mrs Evelyn A.R. Smith
235 L.J. Crumpton-Taylor
236 R. Edwards
237 Mrs J.D. Chessum
238 Mrs J.M. Kippen
239 Mrs K. Barrett
240 Norvil L. Brown
241 P.E. Stevens
242 Hazel Ringer
243 Mrs K. Batis
244 Mrs Janet Gyford
245 D.W. Mackenzie
246 Robert Baldwin
247 H.J. Smith
248 Peter B. Brown
249 Richard M. Brown
250 Stephen Brown
251 Caroline J. Brown
252 Henry Joscelyne Ltd
253 D.C.E. Bailey
254 Mrs M.A. Blower
255 Mrs M. Harrington
256 F.L. Parker
257 David A. Wilcock
258 Mrs P. Thorogood
259 Mrs S.M. Brass
260 J.H.E. Green
261 Barclays Bank Ltd
262 Clifford Sidney Smith
263 Alan F. Daniels
264 Mrs E. Middlebrook
265 David & Janet Possee
266 Richard A. Chapman
267 E.M. Bowtell
268 P.C. Legg
269 P.G. Legg
270 Roland Fisk
271 Hester Bury
272 Warner & Sons Ltd
273 J. Poston
274 Mr & Mrs Poston
275 D. Poston
276 E.M. Wicks
277 F.S. Rogers
278 W.P. Sale
279 Richard Whitbread
280 Gordon E. Messent
281 J.G.F. Moll
282 B.J. Foster
283 John H. Hope
284 285 Mrs M. Burak
286 Sara Nathan
287 Malcolm Bryan
288 D.J. Brisley
289 290 Mrs B.J. Bennett
291 Roy William Livermore
292 293 George H.M. Stutsbury
294 F. Reeves
295 G.A. Brewster
296 W.L. Boyd
297 Leslie S.F. Roberts
298 Braintree Historical Society
299 M.J. Bardell
300 Miss P. Guest
301 Mrs H. Wilcock
302 R.J. Wager
303 John Frederick Parsons
304 Mrs M. Morley
305 P.D. Sutton
306 307 P.E. Simpson
308 309 D.J. Clark
310 311 A. Mackenzie
312 Mr & Mrs M. Stewart
313 John T. Symonds
314 Alec Hunter High School
315 Andrew R. Plumb
316 Rev Stanley Conway-Lee
317 Mrs P.A. Pickering
318 320 St Michael's School
321 Douglas John Muddiman
322 Great Bradfords Junior School
323 Bocking Church Street School
324 T.R. Harrington
325 Robert G. Green
326 Bettina K. Isaak
327 Joyce H. Robinson
328 R.T. Hutley
329 Essex Record Office
330 Alban Thurston
331 Miss M.J. Richardson
332 Adrian Corder Birch
333 K.L. Amey
334 Brian Watts
335 Betty Childs
336 Nicola Clarke
337 Edgar Brand
338 Ian Woodroffe
339 T. Henderson
340 Andrew Millar
341 Mrs L.F. Bates
342 John Ray Junior School
343 Paul Cooper
344 P.B. Saunders
345 Mrs G. Holmes
346 Robert Francis Hills
347 C.W. Brewer
348 J.M. Hayward
349 Jane Jones
350 Local Studies Librarian
351 Alida A. Butcher
352 Julia MacDermot
353 William H. Emery
354 James Waring
355 Mr & Mrs J.R. Jackson
356 Norman Cresswell
357 Gillian Wiltshire
358 Michael J. Morgan
359 360 Mrs John J. Redfern Jnr
361 C.W. Martin
362 363 Leonard George Dalton
364 Peter J. Chissell
365 393 Essex County Library
394 Crittall & Winterton
395 J. Norman
396 400 J.W. Tyler
401 Donald Cobb
402 Raymond M. Palmer
403 Joan & Geoff Hutchings
404 Ray & Anne Skinner
405 William Clark
406 Peter Charles Carder
407 Frank Gray
408 Judy Herbert
409 R.A. Masheder
410 J.M. Boreham
411 412 R. Goodey
413 Mrs M.G. Evans
414 415 K.R. Sutton
416 S.M. Martin
417 E.G. Playle
418 E.S. Davis
419 Michael Frank Tame
420 421 C.G. Meek
422 N. Peagram
423 Mrs M.E. Game
424 K. Willis
425 Mrs J.E. Coxell
426 Constance Dart
427 J. Melvyn Joscelyne
428 I.D. Brown
429 University of Essex
430 A.J. Croot
431 John James McAuliffe
432 Mrs M.C. Rogers
433 Mrs J.N.R. Dickinson
434 E.C. Williams
435 Braintree & Bocking
436 Heritage Trust
437 D.J. Amos
438 Murkin Family
439 P.T. Young
440 Miss K.M. Taylor
441 Mrs C.E. Grout
442 P. Oliver
443 T. Corsham
444 M.P. Shaw
445 446 J.W. Nunn
447 Peter William Thorogood
448 449 Mrs Bennett
450 451 Mrs O.E. Downham
452 Mrs E.J. Burden
453 Mrs S. Warner
454 Mrs K. Bowtell
455 Mrs M.G. Barnard
456 Mrs Angela Comfort
457 P.R. Hale
458 Mrs L. Tame
459 R.H. Perkin
460 John Chapman
461 B. Cook
462 M.A. Herbert
463 Mr & Mrs R.A. Herbert

464 W.E. Drew
465 Miss M. Thompson
466 Dorothy Cook
467 R.A. Watson
468 Cllr J.M. Lyon
469 Edward A.J. Williams
470 S.R.J. Ashby
471 M.P. Wilkins
472 Mr & Mrs Douglas Baker
473 Mr & Mrs J. Webb
474 F.S. Woodroffe
475 H.M. Stuchfield
476 Mrs B. Owen
477 Mr & Mrs D. Moore
478 Mrs M.E. Sanders
479 Mr & Mrs E.C.P. Brand
480 V.J. Barnard
481 Mrs I.M. Underwood
482 Andrew Phillips
483 Evelyn Dorothy Easter
484 M.W. Young
485 Beryl Ricketts
486 C.E. Rayner
487 P.S. Bardell
488 K.W. Gill
489 Jacobs Family
490 D.D. Riddle
491 Technical Panel Industries
492 Anthony P. Pudney
493 Ian Thorogood
494 D.J. Knight
495 D.J. Croot
496 Lawrence Makin
497 Miss Doris R. Blyth
498 M. Taylor
499 Sidney Ernest Clarke
500 The Braintree & Bocking Heritage Trust Competition 1981 Prizewinners: Sister Mary Cuthbert
501 BBHTC 1981: The Friends of Bradford Street
502 BBHTC 1981: John Bunyan Junior School
503 BBHTC 1981: Robert Long
504 BBHTC 1981: Prize-winning entry from Braintree, Mass., USA
505
508 Christine Wicks
509 Mrs J.E. Goodwin
510 L. Williams
511 S.D. Pryke
512 D.E. Draysey
513 Mrs Mason
514 W. Kimmings
515 R.K. Spalding
516 Rowland Eric Game
517 G. Wright
518 Edward Alister Childs
519 Mrs M.P. Hills
520 Mr & Mrs W.G. Robathan
521 Charles Woodroffe
522 Michael L. Makin
523 Miss J. Partridge
524 D.G.W. Spinks
525 Mrs R.P. Goody
526 Mrs E. Whitehead
527 Mrs J. Barulis
528 Mrs Daphne Ives
529 Krystyna Singleton
530 Nancy Clare Cribbin
531 John Armistead
532 Chrissy Robathan
533 Henry Joscelyne Ltd
534 Mrs Daines

Remaining names unlisted

KEY TO CAPTION CREDITS

CB	Clive Birch
CR	Christine Robathan
DAB	D. A. Baker
DW	D. Wilcock
ERO	Essex Records Office
HW	Mrs H. Wilcock
JA	John Armistead
NG	Nicki Gowers
VL	Vic Lewis
WA	The Archive of Warner & Son Ltd

1 Vivienne Loomes; 2 Catherine Cockburn; 3 Don Thompson; 4 Susan Harper; 5 Vic Lewis; 6 W Argus of Rebma (owned by V. Lewis); 7 Keith Briggs; 8 Frank Reading; 9 Martin Brown; 10 Jitendra Desai; 11 Jim Collins; 12 Bill Cotton; 13 David Bowtell; 14 Ron Hawkins; 15 George Wright; 16 Andrew McLeod; 17 Ian Awde; 18 T. Cheung; 19 Len Lane; 20 Eric Gill; 21 Gordon Twitchett; 22 L. Hamilton Joscelyne MBE JP; 23 Melvyn Joscelyne; 24 Chief Inspector Pudney; 25 Frank Wright (Chairman of Chamber of Trade) 26 Norman Perry; 27 George Posner; 28 Ray Lovell; 29 Jim Townrow; 30 Keith Ingall; 31 Robin Addington; 32 Richard Townrow; 33 Robert Swain; 34 Norman Schofield; 35 George Savage JP; 36 Ron Olley; 37 Kit Barton; 38 Brian Rowley; 39 Nelson Moody; 40 Mike Ware; 41 Wynford Lloyd; 42 Geoff Nicholls; 43 Road Sweeper; 44 Vic Butcher; 45 Ken Brown; 46 unknown soldier; 47 Robert Smith; 48 Richard Groves TD; 49 Vic Smith; 50 Alex Turner; 51 Bill Reading; 52 Peter Hutton; 53 Lance Goodwin; 54 Brian Joscelyne; 55 Ben Joscelyne; 56 Peter Nicholls; 57 Chris Goodwin; 58 Ron Digby; 59 Phillip Osborne; 60 Robert Goodwin; 61 newsboy Ernie Lockwood; 62 Don Osborne; 63 Maurice Young; 64 George Shiffner; 65 Jim Smith; 66 Tigger (Peter Hutton's dog); 67 Albany Wiseman FSIAD.

ENDPAPERS: FRONT—Braintree and Bocking from Chapman and André's Map of Essex, 1777. (ERO/JA) BACK—Braintree Parish from Tithe Map, 1840. (ERO)

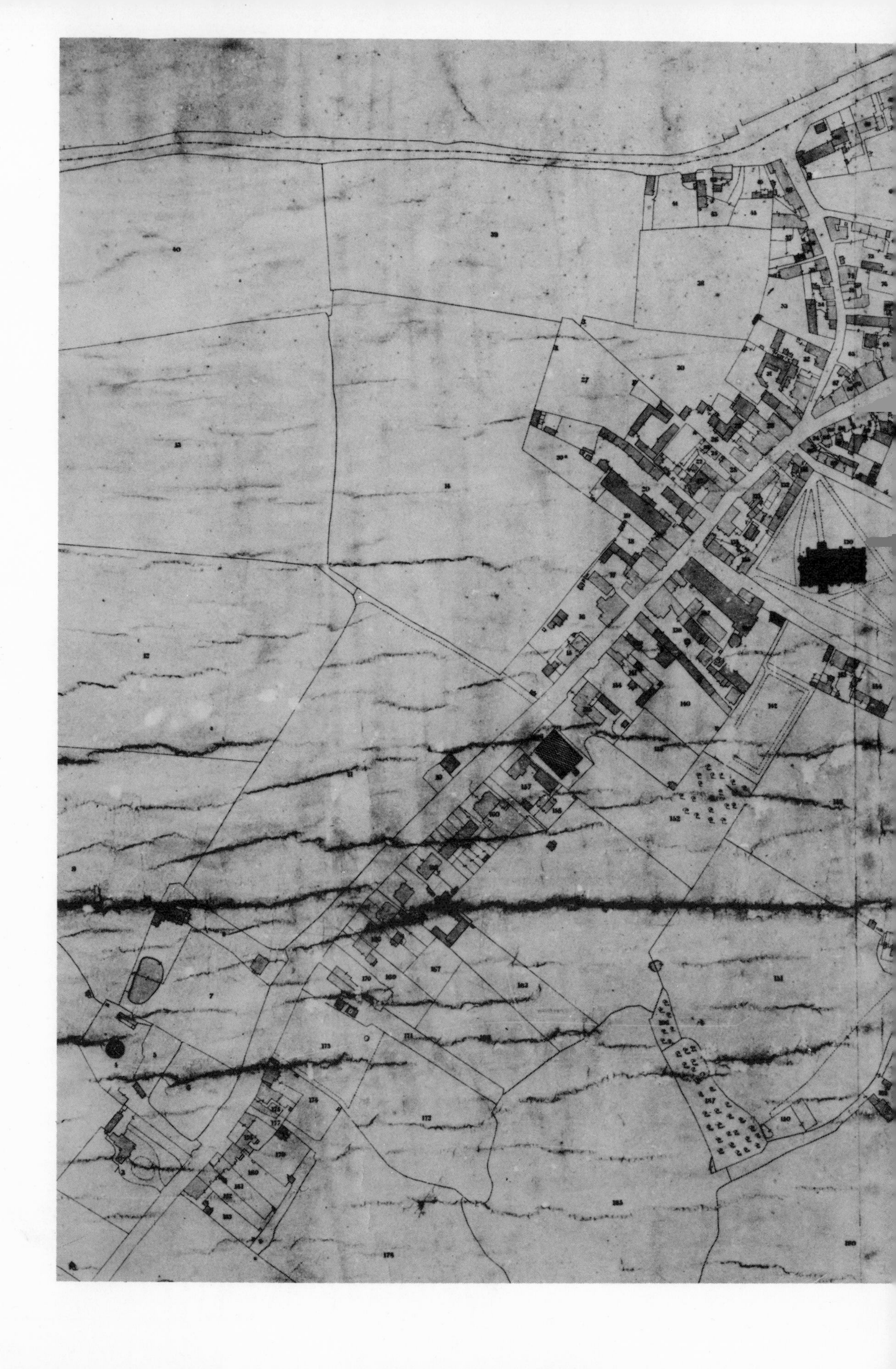